THE WRITER'S
BLOCK

186 IDEAS TO JUMP-START
YOUR IMAGINATION

by Jason Rekulak

RUNNING PRESS
PHILADELPHIA · LONDON

Library of Congress Cataloging-in-Publication Number 00-134984

ISBN 0-7624-0948-7

Edited by Melissa Wagner
Interior design by Terry Peterson
Cover design by Bill Jones

This book may be ordered by mail from the publisher.
Please include $2.50 for postage and handling.
But try your bookstore first!

Running Press Book Publishers
125 South Twenty-second Street
Philadelphia, Pennsylvania 19103-4399

Visit us on the web!
www.runningpress.com

Introduction

"Every writer I know
has trouble writing."

—*Joseph Heller*

During the years I've worked as an editor, I have teamed up with authors of all different ages, abilities, and experience. But whenever people ask me about writer's block, one particular incident always comes to mind,

and I want to begin this book by telling you about it.

Just a few weeks into 1999, I went to my office inbox and found an envelope addressed to Hans Christian Andersen. At first, I thought our mail room had made a mistake. But then I flipped through my company's catalog and learned that we once published an illustrated edition of Andersen's classic fairy tales. So I opened the envelope and began to read. Here is the letter in its entirety (with misspellings and grammatical errors intact):

Dear Hans Christen Anderson,
I was wondering if you made the stories in your book and which story you liked best. I think that the book Thumbelina is the best, plus Thumbelina is my favorite fairy tale book. I was even planning to write my own book, too! I grew very excited when I thought of that. After a few days I reconized it was hard, but I didn't get it. If I already wrote a book a long time ago (that was called "Sleep over Party," and was a few pages long) why can't I just do it? If you know how to get ready to write a book, can you tell me? PLEASE WRITE BACK.

Yours sincerely,
Kathy Stanton

Now Kathy Stanton (I've changed her name) is probably eight or nine years old, and has no intention to write the Great American Novel. She's not concerned about symbolism or structure or plot or the reaction of friends, families, and critics. She's simply writing to entertain herself, and already she has learned (and expressed!) a simple truth: Writing is hard. Writing is hard *for everyone*. We all get stuck. Every short story and novel presents its own unique set of challenges, and a writer encounters them for the first time with every new project.

Some people develop writer's block halfway through a first draft—they find themselves in

the middle of a short story and discover that they're stuck. The words just won't come; perhaps they're starting to lose interest in their characters, or feel that the plot suddenly seems contrived. Other people claim to live in a perpetual state of writer's block. They say they want to be writers, but they're waiting for inspiration to strike, or for a really good idea to sink their teeth into.

This book offers solutions to all different kinds of writer's block, but it is not a how-to manual. There is so much contradictory advice within these pages, I don't think a how-to manual on writing could ever be written. Frederick Forsyth says, "Write about what you

know," and Ken Kesey says, "Write about what you don't know." Isak Dinesen let her characters run wild and "take over" the story; Vladimir Nabokov refers to his characters as "galley slaves." Ernest Hemingway says talent is a necessity; Gordon Lish says talent is irrelevant. The contradictions go on and on and on.

All we can really do is look at techniques that have worked for others, and choose techniques that work for us. And write. Write every day. Write with all you've got, using every resource at your disposal. I believe that inspiration can be found anywhere—in dreams, highway billboards, newspaper personal ads, the Yellow Pages, restaurant menus, family

photo albums, and bizarre morning TV talk shows. There's always something to write about. Or, as Fyodor Dostoevsky put it, "There is no subject so old that something new cannot be said about it."

Aside from this introduction, *The Writer's Block* is not meant to be read in a linear fashion. Rather, I hope you will keep it alongside your dictionary and thesaurus, and refer to it whenever your imagination runs dry. Sometimes writer's block is nothing more than an indication that you should put your current project on hold, and move on to something new. This book is designed to make the "something new" process easier.

Whenever your creativity is running low, just pick up *The Writer's Block* (and maybe give it a good shake for luck, á la the Magic 8-Ball) and open to any spread at random. There are three different types of exercises spaced throughout this book:

Writing Challenges: These short assignments are designed to get you writing as quickly as possible; don't ponder the exercise for more than a minute or so before putting pen to paper. With all of these exercises, it's more helpful to *think as you write*—you can always go back and revise it later. The novelist Don DeLillo describes writing as

"a concentrated form of thinking," and once observed, "I don't know what I think about certain subjects, even today, until I sit down and try to write about them." You should use the same approach; resist the urge to plan, outline, chart, or map, and just get the pen moving.

All of these exercises are paired with photographs. For example, the charge "Describe your first brush with danger" is accompanied by a photograph of a boy playing with matches. Some writers may answer this challenge with an autobiographical piece; others may choose to write about the boy in the photograph. Either approach is okay. And perhaps

you'll want to develop the exercise into a longer piece. What begins as a short story about trespassing or shoplifting could potentially develop into a complete novella about your parents' divorce. Welcome these kinds of changes, and remember that each exercise is only a jumping-off point; if your story veers into new terrain, consider yourself blessed and stay along for the ride.

Spark Words: Many spreads throughout this book consist of a single word that is paired with a photograph (or photographs). These "spark words" carry different meanings for different people; ask ten different women to write

about the word "diet," for example, and you'll receive ten very different responses. Words like "in-laws," "polygamy," and "pillow talk" provoke equally varied responses.

Other spark words offer direct challenges to your imagination. Can you write a scene or story that centers around words like "Oops" or "Ouch?" How about the word "Viagra?" I can hear your mental gears spinning already. Just remember: As with the exercises, you shouldn't plan very long before setting pen to paper. And you should only treat these spark words as a jumping-off point—follow the story into new territory if that's where it wants to go. By obeying the lead of your imagination, you

may end up with a perfectly wonderful short story that doesn't mention the original spark word once.

Writing Topics: From choosing a title and selecting an opening line to coping with negative criticism, these topics feature advice and exercises from legendary and contemporary writers. Want to know where Barbara Kingsolver finds the outrageous names for her characters? It's in this book. If you want to know why Isabel Allende begins every one of her novels on January 8th, you'll learn that, too. And you'll hear from Mary Higgins Clark about the three deadly words no writer should

have in their vocabulary. When appropriate, these topics conclude with a related exercise or writing challenge, but feel free to ignore them if your instincts pull you in another direction. Again, the key here is to let your imagination take the lead.

Whatever happens, just write. Don't second-guess your abilities, don't underestimate your imagination, and don't make excuses. Erskine Caldwell, author of *Tobacco Road*, told one interviewer, "You can always write something. You write limericks. You write a love letter. You do something to get you in the habit of writing again, to bring back the desire."

Perseverance is the name of the game—if you're willing to put in the hours that the craft of writing demands, then you're bound to experience many of its greatest rewards.

If you're interested in further reading about writers and writing, be sure to browse the Selected Bibliography at the end of this book. And if you have success with a particular exercise (or have any comments about *The Writer's Block* in general), I'd love to hear from you via e-mail: jrekulak@hotmail.com. Have fun and good luck!

Acknowledgements

It's not easy producing a 672-page book—even if each page only measures a mere three square inches—so I would like to thank the following friends and co-workers for their assistance. Jennifer Worick conceived the idea for this book, and Terry Peterson is responsible for the beautiful design. Production wizards Bill Luckey and Bryan Hayward take credit for manufacturing the book's unique cube shape, and Melissa Wagner and Molly Jay helped me fine-tune an extremely complicated manuscript. I'm also grateful to Running Press Publisher Buz Teacher, who maintained a

steady commitment to this project, and to all of the following individuals, who offered innumerable suggestions and support: Jeff Whitmore, Melissa Jacobs, Jill Scott, Greg Warrington, Nancy Armstrong, Susan Hom, Victoria Hyun, Amy Kingdom, Marc Frey, Danielle McCole, Anne DeSchryver, Joe Cummins, Ken Bingham, Leslie Kang, Ann Keith Kennedy, Debbie Curtis, Patty Smith, Ann Rittenberg, Carrie McGinnis, and Hannah Thompson. Finally, I'd like to extend a special thank you to Julie Scott, who contributed plenty of ideas and time to this project, even as we both scrambled with last-minute wedding preparations.

Describe your first
brush with danger.

Diet

spark word

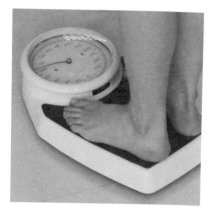

Opening Lines

What makes a good opening line? It depends on the story. Editors of suspense thrillers often hold manuscripts up to an "Airport Test": If you were browsing through an airport bookstore, picked up a paperback, and read the opening line, would you buy the book before boarding your flight? You'll find that John Grisham's novels pass this test nearly every time. His fifth consecutive bestseller, *The Chamber*, begins with this whopper: "The decision to bomb the office of the radical Jew lawyer was reached with relative ease."

But you don't always need to drop bombshells on page one. Ayn Rand's epic *Atlas Shrugged* starts by posing a question: "Who is John Galt?" Alice Walker's *The Color Purple* opens with a warning: "You better not never tell nobody but God." And William Gibson's *Neuromancer* begins with an arresting image: "The sky above the port was the color of television, tuned to a dead channel."

Draw up a list of five favorite novels and review their opening lines. What drew you in? A beautiful metaphor? The hint of danger? Try duplicating the effect in opening lines of your own. See where they take you.

Write a story about
the images on a roll
of film—using only
12, 24, or 36 paragraphs.

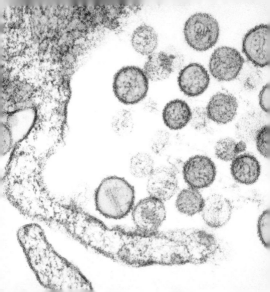

Virus

To Outline or Not to Outline

Outlines are most common among thriller and mystery writers, for obvious reasons. Jeffery Deaver (*The Bone Collector*) claims that the surprising plot twists of his suspense novels wouldn't be possible unless he plotted out all of the details in advance; he usually spends eight months researching and writing the outline, and four months writing the manuscript itself. But non-genre writers use outlines, too. John Barth wrote, "I don't see how anybody starts a novel without knowing how it's going to end. I usually make detailed outlines: how many chapters it will be and so forth." On the other

side of the fence are writers who prefer a more organic approach to their craft; Aldous Huxley wrote, "I know very dimly when I start what's going to happen. I just have a very general idea, and then the thing develops as I write."

If you're suffering from writer's block, try changing your approach. Make a detailed outline of the story—or plunge headfirst into the opening paragraph without any idea where you're going. Either way, the change in routine may be surprisingly effective.

Tell the story of a job interview that goes badly.

The more your character wants the job, the better the story will be.

Sibling Rivalry

Barbara Kingsolver achieved international success with novels like *The Bean Trees*, *Animal Dreams*, and *The Poisonwood Bible*. At readings and lectures, she is frequently asked where she finds the names for her characters (who often have distinctive monikers like Turtle, Loyd, Oreanna, Rose-Johnny, Newt Hardbine, and Annawake Fourkiller). Kingsolver explains, "I give almost as much thought to the naming of my principal characters as I did for my children." In fact, the names of Halimeda and Cosima Noline (the two sisters in *Animal Dreams*) came straight out of a "Name Your Baby" book that Kingsolver references while developing her

characters. These books are inexpensive and invaluable references for the fiction writer, because they're loaded with useful information about the origins and derivations of common names. More importantly, they also contain hundreds of *uncommon* names—great names like Ramona and Cormac and Octavia—that will help lend your character a sense of individuality.

Create a new character from scratch by beginning with the name first. Write as much as you know about him or her, and let the character carry you into a story.

According to officials at Graceland,

Elvis Presley receives an estimated

one hundred valentines every year.

Write a story about one.

Trespass

BEWARE
OF
DOG

The World's Shortest Stories

Since 1987, the *New Times* in San Luis Obispo, California has sponsored an annual contest for "Fifty-Five Fiction." These are short stories which must be—I kid you not—fifty-five words or less. Sounds impossible, right? That's what I thought, until I read a winning entry that was penned by my good pal Jeff Whitmore:

Bedtime Story

"Careful, honey, it's loaded," he said, re-entering the bedroom.

Her back rested against the headboard. "This for your wife?"

"No. Too chancy. I'm hiring a professional."

"How about me?"

He smirked. "Cute. But who'd be dumb enough to hire a lady hit man?"

She wet her lips, sighting along the barrel.

"Your wife."

Jeff's story has it all—suspense, sex, betrayal, revenge, and murder—in a mere fifty-three words! Attempting one of these super-short stories is a valuable lesson in the economy of language—notice how much of Jeff's story is suggested, from the relationship between the characters to the gun itself. With this model in mind, craft your own story of fifty-five words or less.

Write an argument
between two characters
that begins in bed.

Halloween

Must-Read TV

This exercise offers you the rare chance to both write and watch TV—which may explain why it's so popular with college creative writing students. Here's how it works: Put a blank tape in your VCR and record a TV sitcom that you've never watched before (ideally, you should know nothing about the characters or premise). Mute the volume on your TV and watch with a notepad in hand. Make up dialogue for all of the characters and jot down names for them. Invent the central plot or situation based on the visual cues you receive. Watch the entire episode, then sit down with

your notes and channel them into some kind of fiction.

This exercise is especially fun to try as a group, because other writers have a great time trying to recognize the genesis of each story. And after you're finished, be sure you go back and watch the taped episode with sound. Given the amount of junk on TV nowadays, you'll probably make a substantial improvement over the original program!

Take revenge on your least favorite teacher in high school. Write a character sketch that exposes his or her flaws.

Write About Your Pets

Why not? Some beginners might be reluctant to use their pets as material, thinking that "animal stories" are strictly for kids. But look at the wealth of evidence to the contrary: John Steinbeck chronicled his cross-country journey with an "old French gentleman poodle" in *Travels with Charley*, and Virginia Woolf imagined the life of a cocker spaniel in the short novel *Flush*. More recently, Lilian Jackson Braun has experienced a phenomenal success with *The Cat Who . . .* mystery series, in which a quartet of felines help newspaper writer Jim Qwilleran solve a series of crimes.

Cormac McCarthy described the life of a she-wolf in *The Crossing*, and Paul Auster wrote an entire novel from the point-of-view of a dog in *Timbuktu*.

So write about your cat or dog (or hamster, or snake, or tarantula). Perhaps, like Auster, you'll even take the risk of writing from the animal's point-of-view. Just remember how much you loved *Watership Down* or *The Call of the Wild*, and you should do fine!

Imagine that you could wake up tomorrow in someone else's body. Whose would it be? How would your life change? What are some of the first things you'd do?

P.O.W.

Take a Writing Vacation

If you're really agonizing over writer's block—that is, if you break into a cold sweat just from the very *thought* of writing—then you need to take extreme measures. Make a conscious decision not to do any writing—or any creative work, period—for one week. This may seem like odd advice for someone who wants to write, but the results are twofold. First, you'll stop feeling stressed out because you'll have given yourself permission not to write. Secondly, and more importantly, you'll allow your "creative well" to be replenished. Psychologists tell us that the subconscious

mind works twenty-four hours a day; every time you leave your house, stories are happening all around you, and the mind stores these arbitrary details, conversations, and confrontations in a literary equivalent of a compost pile. While you're idling away on the beach or at the movies, your subconscious will already be starting on your next scene or short story. And when the end of the week is up, you can return to your desk and start transferring these ideas to paper.

Write about a
near-death
experience.

Homeless

Don DeLillo achieved international acclaim for novels like *Libra*, *Underworld*, and *White Noise* (winner of the 1985 National Book Award), and it's hard to think of a writer who pays more attention to word choice, grammar, and sentence structure. DeLillo's attention to detail is so meticulous, in fact, that he often focuses on his work "one paragraph at a time." He told *The Paris Review*, "When I was working on *The Names* I devised a new method—new to me, anyway. When I finished a paragraph, even a three-line paragraph, I automatically went to a fresh page to start the new paragraph. No crowded pages. This enabled me to see a given set of sentences

more clearly. It made rewriting easier and more effective. The white space on the page helped me concentrate more deeply on what I'd written." This approach is useful to anyone suffering from writer's block—rather than focusing to finish a story or chapter or novel, simply concentrate on producing one good paragraph at a time. The rest may take care of itself.

Describe a time you peeked in someone's diary.

What did it reveal to you
about the person?

How did you feel
about yourself?

D.W. I.

Most Likely to Succeed

Many writers seem to have a rough time in high school—how else can you explain the frustrated teenage protagonists of novels like *A Separate Peace* or *The Catcher in the Rye*? The good news is, the most exhilarating—and embarrassing—moments of adolescence can be channeled into great fiction, and you can summon the memories just by opening your Senior Class yearbook. Imagine what happened to "Most Likely to Succeed" and "Most Popular." Write about the class clown who defied everyone's expectations and became a celebrity. Tell us which of your former teach-

ers initiated an affair with one of his or her students. Show us the secret life of the Cafeteria Lunch Lady. Relive the glacial passing of time in a high school detention session, or the petty jealousies involved in the planning of the school musical.

Use as many of your own high school memories as you wish, but feel free to embellish or alter "the truth" as you go along. Personal revenge fantasies that involve "Most Popular" are also permitted.

Write a story set in the 1980s.

Use as many period
elements as you can.

Traffic Jam

spark word

Real People

Pat Conroy hit bestseller lists with his novel *The Prince of Tides*—but Conroy's sister recognized so much of herself in the story that she never spoke to her brother again. This kind of family reaction is a serious concern for many of us, and often the fear will develop into full-blown writer's block. After all, how can you write honestly about the failings of your father, if you're certain he'll recognize himself in your manuscript? Thankfully, there are simple techniques for disguising any real-life individuals who inspire your fiction. You can modify or exaggerate a person's physical

appearance—give Dad an extra thirty pounds, perhaps, or change the color of Mom's hair. Changing their occupations is another good idea—many people define themselves almost exclusively by their careers. Also feel free to blur or change the relationships among your characters. If you're writing very auto-biographical fiction, the character of your sister could easily be a roommate, cousin, best friend, or co-worker. Your father could appear in the guise of a boss, neighbor, teacher, or shopkeeper. By consciously altering the truth, you'll actually develop your characters into more "real" fictional creations.

Since 1980, more than fifty forgeries have been discovered at New York's Metropolitan Museum of Art. Write about one of them.

Extreme Imitation

When Ethan Canin was an engineering major at Stanford University, he discovered the short stories of John Cheever—and the course of his life was changed forever. In an interview with *The Writer* magazine, Canin explained that he would literally type out Cheever's stories, just to feel what it was like to have "written" them. "It's interesting because you learn things," Canin explained. "Something simple about Cheever is that his paragraphs are longer than yours would have been. His sentences are longer. He pushes everything farther than I would have pushed them."

Take a favorite passage from one of your favorite books, and type it into your word processor. Most of the influences on your writing are processed through your mental facilities, but this is an opportunity to sift an author's words through your own hands, to feel a fraction of what Flannery O'Connor or Raymond Chandler might have felt as they completed the final typewritten drafts of their masterpieces.

Write about
the biggest
secret that you
failed to keep.

Custody

John Irving has enjoyed a success that most writers only dream of; most of his novels (like *The World According to Garp* and *The Cider House Rules*) are embraced by critics and spend months on hardcover bestseller lists. When asked by the *New York Times* how he goes about writing his novels, Irving explained that he usually writes his last sentences first: "I always begin at the ending...[Writers] know more about their books when they begin them than they think they know. If a writer can't see the end, I can't imagine how he can feel purposeful enough to begin." Although this method contradicts the approach of many other writers (who claim to

discover their stories as they write them), it has certainly worked wonders for Irving, and might benefit you, too. If you're stuck for a good last line to start with, use this one (courtesy of Irving's second novel, *The Water-Method Man*): "Mindful of his scars, his old harpoons and things, Bogus Trumper smiled cautiously at all the good flesh around him."

Visit a nearby cemetery—the older, the better. Sit down beside the most unusual tombstone you can find, and write about the person lying underneath you.

Greed

Interrogate Your Characters

Novelist and playwright Ken Bingham heads one of the most popular creative writing workshops in Philadelphia, and he advocates "asking questions" as a means of avoiding writer's block. Whenever one of his students becomes stuck, Ken proceeds with an inquisition about the main character. The first few questions concern simple traits like age, race, place of birth, occupation, and education. But the subsequent questions are increasingly revealing: "Who has the character telephoned at three o'clock in the morning? The local talk radio station? Their ex-wife from fifteen years ago?" Another good one:

"Tell me about a time when your character intentionally set out to hurt someone—and tell me why." Bingham doesn't allow his students to say "I don't know" or "My character would never do that." He forces them to invent a scenario in which the character *would* do that—and these scenarios are often the seeds of great short stories.

If you're blocked, ask yourself how well you know your main character. What are three secrets they would never tell anyone? What pushes your character's buttons? Start asking questions, and you may find it hard to stop.

Write a story
set in the
kitchen of
a fast-food
restaurant.

Pillow Talk

Write What You Know?

It's the most common advice a beginning writer is likely to hear. By writing about one's own experiences, a person can create genuine, honest fiction that feels "real." But E. Annie Proulx calls this "the most tiresome and stupid advice that could possibly be given," and defended her position by saying, "If we write simply about what we know we never grow. We don't develop any facility for languages, or an interest in others, or a desire to travel and explore and face experience head-on. We just coil tighter and tighter into our boring little selves. What one should write about

is what interests one." Cynthia Ozick agrees with her: "The world is bigger and wider and more complex than our small subjective selves. One should prod, goad the imagination." Perhaps the most balanced advice on the subject comes from Irish novelist Colum McCann, who encourages writers to "Write about what you don't know and discover what you do know. Ultimately you can only write about what you know, but confronting what you supposedly don't know can be very liberating."

According to the National Coffee Organization, there are more than 300,000 Americans who consume at least ten cups of coffee each day. Describe one of these people.

Chronicle the longest amount of time you've ever gone without sleeping.

Orson Scott Card is one of the leading voices in science fiction—and the first writer to receive both the Hugo and the Nebula awards for best novel, two years in a row! (The winning works were 1986's *Ender's Game* and its sequel, *Speaker for the Dead*). In an interview with the website Writers Write, Card advised, "Don't even think about writing science fiction or fantasy unless you've read every story in: *The Hugo Winners, The Science Fiction Hall of Fame, Dangerous Visions,* and *Again, Dangerous Visions.* These stories are the root of the field. If you don't know them, you will try to reinvent the wheel; and since the readers do know them, it will kill your work."

Although a solid familiarity with existing science fiction is essential, you don't need to have a college degree in science. Articles in mainstream magazines like *Discover* or *National Geographic* might be enough to spark your imagination. Look for the latest development in an area that interests you (Bio-ethics? E-mail viruses? Life on Mars?) and start writing about it.

If you've ever said,

"I wish I was a fly

on the wall for *that*

conversation,"

write about what

you might have seen

or heard.

Short Fuse

spark word

Bizarre Books

E. Annie Proulx credits the inspiration for her Pulitzer prize-winning novel, *The Shipping News*, to *The Ashley Book of Knots*, an obscure little book that she bought at a garage sale for twenty-five cents (fans of *The Shipping News* will remember that the story contains dozens of references to hitches, lanyards, ropes, and other knotty subjects). After learning this, I began paying closer attention to the dusty hardcovers at antique stores and flea markets, and you might do the same.

Some of the best oddball titles are discussed in Russell Ash's and Brian Lake's *Bizarre Books*

(Pavilion, 1998), which highlights unusual tomes like *Who's Who in Barbed Wire* (Rabbit Ear Press, 1970); *The Romance of Rayon* (Whittaker and Robinson, 1933); *I Was Hitler's Maid* (Long, 1940); *Atomic Bombing: How to Protect Yourself* (William H. Wise and Co., 1950); and even *The Joy of Chickens* (Prentice-Hall, 1981), a history and celebration of poultry. Don't laugh: If a book on tying knots can spark E. Annie Proulx's imagination, there's no telling what might work for you!

Write about your first
artistic expression.

Chain Reaction

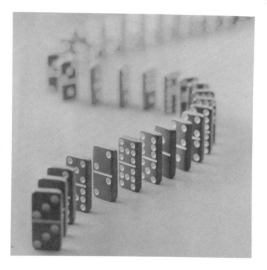

The Horror, The Horror

Editors place a considerable distinction between thrillers, in which the antagonist is human (typically a serial killer), and horror novels, in which the antagonist is supernatural—a ghost, a witch, a demonically possessed Plymouth Fury, and so on. Horror fiction has never received much respect from critics, but it's hard to deny the power (and literary achievement) of masterpieces like Ira Levin's *Rosemary's Baby*, William Peter Blatty's *The Exorcist*, and Shirley Jackson's *The Haunting of Hill House*. Over the last two decades, Hollywood special effects have inspired all

kinds of gory, overblown passages in contemporary horror fiction, but the best writers remember that subtlety is key (in Stephen King's *Bag of Bones*, for example, a ghost communicates using the magnetic letters on a refrigerator; in *Rosemary's Baby*, we suspect that benign rites of maternity are becoming corrupted by witchcraft and satanism . . . or are they?)

Write a story that contains an element of the supernatural but keep it subtle. Don't go for the gross-out; instead, aim to raise the hairs on the back of your reader's neck.

Describe the most disappointing gift you've ever received.

What did the gift reveal about the giver?

Accident-prone

Physical Limitations

I know plenty of writers who love coming down with a cold or the flu, because it gives them the perfect excuse to stay home and focus on their fiction. When else will you find so much uninterrupted time to spend with your characters? Professional journalists understand that fatigue, illness, and the lack of so-called "inspiration" have nothing to do with good writing—a deadline is a deadline, and the work must be done. Garrison Keillor put it another way: "You can write comedy when you're sick, when you're lonely as a barn owl and your head hurts and your friends are mad

at you. It's just work, that's all, and you go do it if you need to." Don't allow the limitations of your physical condition to interfere with your mind; don't make excuses for yourself. And if you want to make physical limitations work *for* you, consider this advice from crime writer Charles Willeford. Never allow yourself to take a leak in the morning until you've written a page. That way you're guaranteed a page a day, and at the end of a year you have a novel."

Write about a
parent trying
to explain
the facts of life
to his or her child.

Amy Tan hit bestseller lists with her first novel, *The Joy Luck Club*, and followed it up with two more successes, *The Kitchen God's Wife* and *The Hundred Secret Senses*. In an interview with the *Sonoma Independent* newspaper, Tan attributed her storytelling skills to both of her parents: "[My father] was a Baptist minister and his idea of quality time with his children—since he worked seven days a week—was to read his sermons aloud to me and see what I thought. . . . Stories from my mother came more naturally, and I'd listen as she and my aunts sat at a table covered with newspapers, shelling fava beans or chopping vegetables and gossiping about the family."

Take the reader behind
the wheel with the worst
driver you've ever known.

Think back to a particularly memorable story that your mother or father told you. How would you describe their storytelling skills? And how did these early lessons in form influence your own work? Put their tale into words, and make a conscious effort to be faithful to the original storyteller's approach.

Heist

Change Would Do You Good

If you're having trouble getting started, determine what is changing in your characters' lives. Some of the most memorable novels begin with characters who must face alterations in their lifestyles. In the first few pages of Stephen King's *Bag of Bones*, we learn that the narrator's wife has just died in a freak car accident. In the first chapter of Anne Tyler's *The Accidental Tourist*, Macon Leary learns that his wife wants a divorce. At the start of Harper Lee's *To Kill a Mockingbird*, Scout learns that there's a new boy, Dil, in the neighborhood. And as Barbara Kingsolver's *The Bean Trees*

opens, a young woman finds herself the unexpected caretaker of an abandoned baby.

Change forces your characters to make decisions about a situation. And the way they handle a situation will shape how we feel about them. If the characters in your manuscript are simply plodding through the story, throw a curve ball into their lives. As the Sheryl Crow song goes, "A change would do you good."

Think of a person you don't like, and describe what you might say if you had to share an elevator ride together.

Then describe what

happens when the

elevator breaks down.

For six hours.

Magic

Stories From The Tube

I've known writers who draw their inspiration from a wide range of sources—family histories, natural wonders, passages from scripture, scientific phenomenon. Yet Matthew Sharpe is the first writer I've known to derive his inspiration from TV commercials. The ten stories in his debut collection, *Stories from the Tube*, borrow elements of their plots from commercials for deodorant, coffee, automobiles, and other familiar products. The story "Tide," for example, begins with an excerpt from a television commercial shooting script:

A mother and her small daughter open the trunk of a car to find the daughter's leotard has a red, wet stain on it.

Daughter: And the ballet's tomorrow!

Mother: Honey, we'll get it out.

What follows is a surprisingly moving story about parenthood, ballet, menstruation, and a broken bottle of grape juice—it's all much more literary than anything produced by a Madison Avenue advertising agency! For a fun, off-the-wall exercise, watch a half hour of television and jot down one-line descriptions of the commercials. Then, like Sharpe, use any one of the ads as a jumping-off point.

Tell a story that begins with the discovery of a ransom note.

Write a story in the form
of a political apology.

Flirting

E. Annie Proulx is quick to admit that a great deal of research goes into her novels, which include best-selling books like *Postcards*, *Accordion Crimes*, and the Pulitzer Prize-winning *The Shipping News*. But this doesn't mean that Proulx spends all of her time in libraries. "The digging involves more than books," she wrote in an essay on inspiration for the *New York Times*. "I need to know which mushrooms smell like maraschino cherries and which like dead rats." She's also an avid explorer of back roads, and a frequent visitor to garage sales and estate sales, which can serve as a treasure trove of inspiration.

Visit a local garage sale and focus on an

unusual treasure that reveals something about its owner. Maybe it's an obscure book, a threadbare sports jacket, a box of 8-track cassettes, or a distinctive fedora. The more unusual and distinctive, the better. Focus on the history of this object—perhaps you'll choose to begin in the hands of the manufacturer, or the item's original owner. Invent the history behind stains, nicks, dents, and other defects.

Describe the worst time
you've ever put your
foot in your mouth.

Degrees of Intelligence

Mentally challenged narrators have appeared in many of the twentieth century's most celebrated novels, from William Faulkner's *The Sound and the Fury* to Winston Groom's *Forrest Gump*. Daniel Keyes achieved international success with his science fiction novel, *Flowers for Algernon*, which tells the story of a mentally handicapped man who grows smarter as the result of a scientific experiment. Every chapter is told through journal entries; the first line begins, "Dr. Strauss says I shoud rite down what I think and remembir and evrey thing that happins to me from now on." This is a

great literary device; as the novel progresses, the narrator becomes progressively smarter, but we're never actually told this information. Instead, we see his intelligence reflected in his improved grammar, spelling, punctuation, and sentence construction.

Flip to any of the exercises within *The Writer's Block*, and address the challenge from the point-of-view of someone who is mentally handicapped. Use their writing ability (or lack thereof) to suggest the degree of their intelligence.

Seventeen percent
of Americans
claim they have
witnessed a ghost.

Describe one of their
encounters . . . or one
of your own.

Fireworks

Culinary Delights

We pause to eat at least three times a day—and yet so many writers neglect the powerful sense of taste. One of the most memorable chapters in Herman Melville's *Moby Dick* is simply called "Chowder," in which Ishmael enjoys a steaming bowl of stew: "It was made of small juicy clams, scarcely bigger than hazel nuts, mixed with pounded ship biscuit, and salted pork cut up into little flakes; the whole enriched with butter, and plentifully seasoned with pepper and salt." More recently, Laura Esquivel had an international bestseller with *Like Water for Chocolate*, a novel that includes

recipes for Quail in Rose Petal Sauce, Northern-style Chorizo, and Cream Fritters. Each chapter begins with a list of ingredients and notes on preparation, which Esquivel weaves seamlessly into the narrative. And Charles Frazier's *Cold Mountain* is practically a primer in country cooking; his characters slaughter hogs, churn apple butter, and cook savory chicken stews.

Write a story or scene that centers around an extraordinary meal. The food itself can be quite simple—even as simple as a TV dinner—but the meal should have an important and lasting significance to the characters.

Describe the youngest baby you've ever held, and how he or she felt in your arms.

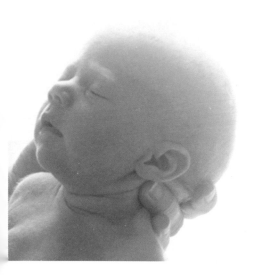

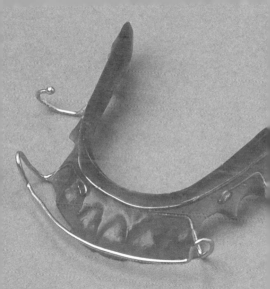

Orthodontics

spark word

David Sedaris has probably held more odd jobs than any writer working today—and while "none of which were the type to hand out tax statements at the end of the year," all have served as useful inspiration for his essays and fiction. In books like *Barrel Fever* and *Naked*, Sedaris chronicles his experiences cleaning houses, picking apples, washing dishes, selling marijuana, writing erotica about "gals who grow to gigantic proportions" for a magazine called *Giantess*, waiting on tables, stripping woodwork, manufacturing jade stash boxes, helping out on a construction site, and (most notably) dressing up as an elf for the Macy's Santaland in New York City. Although

none of these career choices looked great on Sedaris' resume (actually, he probably never even had a resume), they gave him a wealth of experience for his writing. So tell a story about the worst job you've ever had. Or, if you've been lucky in your career choices, write about the worst job you've ever paid anyone to do— and how you felt about paying them to do it.

Write about a graduation
ceremony that was particularly
meaningful for you.

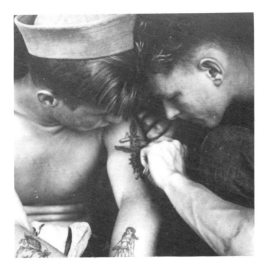

Tattoo

Keep a Dream Journal

A wide range of writers—everyone from Isabel Allende to Spalding Gray and Clive Barker—credit some of their inspiration to an active dream life, and some writers are lucky enough to have entire stories or novels spelled out by their subconscious mind. Robert Louis Stevenson allegedly wrote *Dr. Jekyll and Mr. Hyde* in just three days, after having a vivid nightmare that presented him with the entire plot. Graham Greene claimed that many of his dreams were like serials and that "installments sometimes carry on for weeks and in the end form a whole." Perhaps Amy Tan said it best:

"[I] do feel if ever I was looking for a source of material, all I would have to do is go back to my dreams."

Keep a small notebook beside your bed and, next time you have a particularly vivid dream, force yourself to get up and write about it. Often, dreams that seem spectacular at 3:00 a.m. will seem ludicrous at sunrise—but you still might salvage the spark of an idea that can lead to spectacular fiction.

Write about a time
you've been lost.
Were you in a car?
On foot? In a foreign
country? Alone?

Waiting

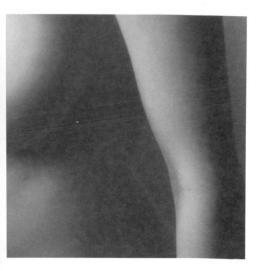

Set a Schedule

If you have trouble writing every day, it helps to set a schedule; you'll find that most authors have pretty regular work habits. Tennessee Williams and Ernest Hemingway began their work at dawn, for example, and James Baldwin started writing when everyone in his house went to sleep. Among more contemporary writers, Mary Gordon writes from 5:30 every morning until 8:00, when the rest of her family awakens. Larry Heinemann and Donald Hall also begin around 5:30. David Sedaris, on the other hand, only writes at night (when asked by an interviewer why he didn't write

earlier, Sedaris replied, "Because it doesn't feel right to drink during the morning.")

Set aside one hour every day to spend at your desk. Honor the appointment no matter what; if the ideas aren't flowing, try one of the other exercises in this book. After just three or four weeks, you should find that your imagination is "primed" and ready to work when you arrive at your desk—and you'll be in the habit to start writing immediately.

Describe your first
encounter with an
illicit substance.

Write about a
beauty pageant—
without using
stereotypes.

J.K. Rowling's series of Harry Potter novels is the biggest publishing phenomenon in years (volume 4, *Harry Potter and the Goblet of Fire*, had the largest first printing in publishing history—3.8 million books in the United States alone). What accounts for this series' astonishing popularity? It may be that young readers identify with Harry Potter, a seemingly "ordinary" kid with no control of his external surroundings—until he learns he has extraordinary magical powers. As Rowling told *Newsweek* magazine, "There will always, always, always be [children's] books about magic, discovering secret powers, stuff that you're not allowed to do. [As a child] there's a

small part of you that wishes you could alter external things to be the way they ought to be."

Children are rarely called upon to make important decisions about their own lives—but some of the very best fiction is about those who do (*The Adventures of Huckleberry Finn* and Russell Banks' *The Rule of the Bone* are just two examples). Write a scene in which a child makes a decision that—wittingly or unwittingly—alters the course of his or her future.

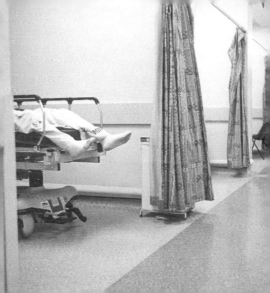

Spend an hour writing in the lobby
of your local emergency room.
Speculate on the circumstances
of those around you.

Marathon

Ten Minutes That Still Make You Cringe

I started working in publishing as an editorial assistant at St. Martin's Press. Once a week or so, a big group of the junior editors would congregate at the Old Town Bar and Grill to flirt, drink beer, and commiserate about the low salaries. Another popular activity was playing a game best described as "Ten Minutes that Still Make You Cringe." In a nutshell, the game consisted of describing the worst thing you'd ever done—the ten minutes of your life that were so shameful or embarrassing, you still cringe just from thinking about them. Most of

the stories were revealed under the influence of alcohol, and I certainly don't plan to reveal any of them here. But if you feel comfortable posing this question to your own friends or co-workers, you'll find yourself sitting on a gold mine of material for good fiction. Or, better yet, pose the question to yourself: What are the ten minutes that still make *you* cringe?

Describe the worst date of your life. Where do you think your date is now? Do you think he or she ever thinks of you?

Massage

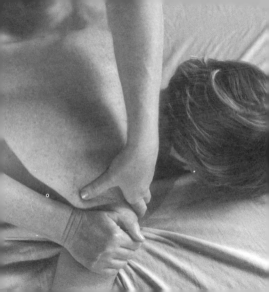

Whatever it Takes

Long before books like *The Writer's Block* existed, writers had to draw their inspiration from any means possible. Agatha Christie claimed she had her best ideas while washing the dishes. Raymond Chandler found inspiration by watching his wife clean house in the nude. Ben Franklin wrote in the bathtub, and Ernest Hemingway liked to write standing up. For many years, Jack Kerouac had a ritual of lighting a candle, writing his poetry, and extinguishing the flame when he was done for the night. Whenever G.K. Chesterton became blocked, he would reach for his bow and fire

arrows through a window that looked out on his backyard. Bertolt Brecht liked to write in pubs, and Truman Capote preferred to write in bed. Some of these approaches are more eccentric than others, but don't let self-consciousness interfere with your need to write. Get in the habit of creating your own writing ritual (cleaning off your desk is a popular one). Then do whatever it takes to get started.

By the early 1990s, more than 30,000 Americans held reservations with Pan Am airlines for a trip to the moon. Write about one of these people.

Cheating

A.S. Byatt won a Booker Prize and international acclaim with her novel *Possession*, a genre-bending story-within-a-story about two young scholars researching a pair of Victorian poets. More recently, she completed *The Matisse Stories*, a trilogy of stories that all concern (at some level) the life and works of the modern French painter. In an interview with *The Writer* magazine, Byatt explained that all three stories developed individually, and linking them together was not her original intention: "It was more that I am totally obsessed with Matisse. He sort of gets into everything I do. He's my touchstone for art, the importance of art, as opposed to anything else, in its purest, most

uncompromising state." Ernest Hemingway was another writer who looked to painters for inspiration; he listed Gauguin, Van Gogh, and Brueghel among his "literary forebears" and once remarked, "I learn as much from painters about how to write as from writers."

Is there a visual artist who influences your work? Perhaps you're mesmerized by the surreal designs of M.C. Escher, or the all-American tableaus of Norman Rockwell, or the abstract still-lifes of Pablo Picasso. Sit down with one of their works, and make a conscious effort to imitate their style with your prose.

Set a small mirror beside your desk and write about your reflection. Describe how you might be perceived by a stranger passing you on the street—what assumptions might he or she make about you, based on your appearance?

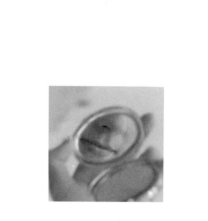

Describe the largest
crowd you've ever
been part of.

Prophecy

Write a story that begins
with the words,

"Why didn't you call me?"

Four Sides to Every Story

Japanese director Akira Kurosawa achieved international acclaim with *Rashomon*, a film that tells the same story four different times —from four different points of view. The plot concerns a young woman, her husband, and a bandit who attacks them. The bandit assaults the woman, but what happens next is open to question; the four different narrators provide wildly different accounts of the aftermath. The film offers valuable lessons in point-of-view, unreliable narrators, and the very idea of omniscience.

Write a scene in which a moving automobile hits a young boy on a bicycle. Describe the

scene four different times, from the following four points-of-view: the driver of the car, a passenger in the car, the child on the bicycle, and a pedestrian who witnesses the accident. You may guide your readers to believe that one of the versions is the "truth," or, like Kurosawa you may allow your readers to decide for themselves, or even question the very notion of "truth."

Red Light District

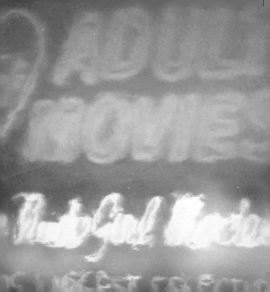

Alarm Clock Openings

It's a common starting point for many of the stories reviewed in a creative writing workshop: An alarm clock sounds. The narrator drags himself to the bathroom and scrutinizes his weary face in the mirror. Then he showers, dresses, grabs the newspaper, and sits down to breakfast. Perhaps he watches television, or has an anxious thought about an important meeting in the afternoon. Meanwhile, the reader of the story is halfway through page four or five, wondering when something interesting is going to happen.

"Alarm Clock Openings" are appealing because they convey a wealth of information

about a character's home, lifestyle, and social standing. Richard Wright's *Native Son* begins with an alarm clock ringing, and we discover that Bigger Thomas lives in a cramped one-room apartment with his mother, brother, and sister. But no less than a minute later, Bigger is bludgeoning a giant rat with a skillet, demonstrating the pent-up aggression that will surface again later in the novel. This scene works because it defies the conventions of a typical morning routine; write your own Alarm Clock Opening that does the same.

Tell a story in the
form of a prayer.

Girl Power

Sex

For some writers, the challenge of a sex scene is no challenge at all (Henry Miller once remarked, "I've led a good rich sexual life, and I don't see why it should be left out."). But most writers approach the subject with some amount of trepidation and self-consciousness. "Sex is difficult to write about because it's just not sexy enough," Toni Morrison has said. "The only way to write about it is not to write much. Let the reader bring his own sexuality into the text." So before you sit down to write that steamy bedroom rendezvous, remember that foreplay is everything (even in the most

controversial erotic novel of the twentieth century, *Lady Chatterley's Lover*, there's more anticipation than copulation.) Avoid blow-by-blow details that make your story read like a sex manual. Remember that personalities are especially crucial here—a sex scene should reveal more about your characters than bare skin. And follow this advice from Mark Helprin as a general rule: "The trick, as with everything else in the world, is to keep it in proportion, to be honest about it, and to be modest."

More than ten million prescription medications are filled incorrectly every year. Write about one of them.

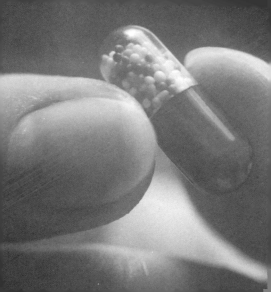

Suits

Read the Novels of Robert James Waller

In the darkest hours of every writer's life, there comes a time when you think to yourself. "I'm wasting my time. I don't have what it takes to be a writer." And in these dark hours, I would encourage you to review the work of Robert James Waller, whose novel *The Bridges of Madison County* stayed at the top of best-seller lists for more than 115 weeks. Warner Books claims that *Bridges* is the best-selling hardcover novel of all time, yet it is full of howlingly bad, clumsily constructed, and downright awful sentences like this one: "He

whispered to her of the visions she brought to him—of blowing sand and magenta winds and brown pelicans riding the backs of dolphins." And this one: "As he moved over her, he alternately kissed her lips or ears or ran his tongue along her neck, licking her as some fine leopard might do in long grass out on the wild. And this one: "[S]he rode on that wind like some temple virgin toward the sweet, compliant fires marking the soft curve of oblivion." For crying out loud—if *this* is the best-selling hardcover novel of all time, why aren't *you* famous by now?

If you were going to be marooned on a deserted island with any one person, who would you want it to be? Write scenes that take place five hours after the shipwreck, five weeks after the shipwreck, and five years after the shipwreck.

Create a paragraph that includes all of the following punctuation symbols: the colon, semi-colon, dash, question mark, parenthesis, and exclamation mark.

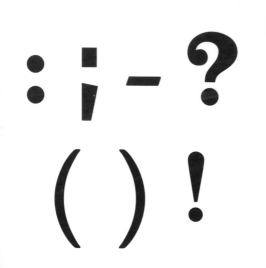

Let Your Fingers
Do the Walking

Most people only reach for the Yellow Pages when they need to order a pizza. But by consciously *reading* the Yellow Pages, you'll stumble across dozens of opportunities for good fiction. While leafing through the Philadelphia 1999–2000 Yellow Pages, I found listings for Dynamite Pest Control ("We Kill Anything That Hops, Skips, or Jumps!"), Good Time Charlie's Escort Service ("Half hour rates available"), and the Firing Line Gun Complex ("Ladies Night Every Tuesday!"). I'm convinced that anyone who visits the Firing Line Gun Complex on

Ladies Night will come away with enough material to write a dazzling short story—maybe even the beginning of a novel.

Open the Yellow Pages and look up any of the following subjects: Guard Dogs, Prosthetic Limbs, Abortion Services/Alternatives, Detective Agencies, Pet Cemeteries, Hair Replacement, and Lawyers (criminal defense and personal injury work best). Use any of these advertisements as the basis for a short story. Write about the veterinary school dropout who opens her own guard dog business. Tell us how anyone gets a job in the prosthetic limb industry. Explore occupations and businesses that are completely unfamiliar to you.

Describe the last time
you were physically
involved in a fight.

Begin a story with
a character who
has lost something
important to them.

Superstitious

Elmore Leonard has written some of the best crime novels of the last twenty years—including *Get Shorty*, *Fifty-Two Pickup*, *Out of Sight*, and *Rum Punch*—and was named a Grand Master by the Mystery Writers of America. He's produced some of the most fully realized characters in contemporary fiction, and has a knack for exploring the psyche of the world's biggest low-lifes. One of my favorite observations by Leonard was mentioned during an interview with the *London Sunday Telegraph*, in which he said, "Criminals are so much more interesting than people up at the country club talking about their golf game or their stocks. All those bad guys have

a mother, too. . . . They worry about what they are going to wear when they commit a crime, I'm sure they do."

Begin a story with a character getting dressed. Be sure to note sizes, designer labels, and any holes or stains in the fabric. A person's choice of clothing will reveal worlds about their motivation, how they perceive themselves, how they want to be perceived by others, and more.

Invent a character who has won 76 million dollars in the Florida State Lottery. What's the first thing they buy? How much do they give to charity? How long before an ex-boyfriend or ex-girlfriend re-enters their lives?

Rediscover a Childhood Favorite

Can you remember the first book you loved as a child? For Rita Dove, it was *Harold and the Purple Crayon*: "Not a great book," she recalls, "but certainly a great book for me because it showed me the possibilities of traveling on the line of one's imagination." When Joyce Carol Oates was eight years old, she would memorize passages from *Alice's Adventures in Wonderland* and recite them throughout her house. Amy Bloom's childhood passions were *A Tale of Two Cities*, *The Scarlet Pimpernel*, and all of the *Superman* comic books. Another

comic book fan was James McBride, who empathized with the plight of Peter Parker (a.k.a. Spiderman): "A lot of his struggles, his trials and tribulations were things I could relate to."

What was the book that first attracted you to reading? Try to remember what elements drew you in. Better yet, go to your library and read the book again. By reconnecting with the stories that attracted you to literature in the first place, you may find just the spark of inspiration you need to proceed.

Flip to any three photographs
in this book at random.

Write a story that
incorporates all of them.

Prom

Be a Dream Date

One of my favorite analogies comes courtesy of Kurt Vonnegut, who taught his students at the University of Iowa that being a good writer is like being a good date. Ask any man or woman to describe the character traits of their "dream date," and they'll be quick to volunteer answers like *intelligent*, *interesting*, *considerate*, *honest*, *funny*, and *attractive*. And of course these words must describe your work. Your stories should be *intelligent* and *interesting*, naturally, but also *considerate*—making unnecessary demands on your reader is like asking your date to pick up the check. If your fiction's not

honest, the reader will be able to tell. And being *funny* never hurt, either—no matter how serious your subject matter, there's probably room for a little levity, ironic or otherwise. Finally, the manuscript itself should be *attractive*, and this means nothing more than double-spacing the text and using one-inch margins all around. So if you're having trouble with a story, make a list of what you would look for in a good date—and make sure that your fiction fits the bill.

Tell the story of a blind
date. Begin writing from
one person's point-of-view.
If you get stuck, switch
to the perspective
of their date.

Describe the most boring job
you've ever suffered through.

Five Great Movies About Writer's Block

Rent 'em and commiserate with the miserable writers on-screen:

1. *The Shining* (1980): Jack Nicholson spends the winter with his family at the creepy Overlook Hotel, so he can finish his novel (instead, he ends up chasing them with an axe). All work and no play makes Jack a dull boy!

2. *Barton Fink* (1991): Joel and Ethan Coen wrote and directed this 1930s period piece about a successful playwright (Jon Turturro) who experiences writer's block after he's lured to Hollywood to write wrestling scripts.

3. *Shakespeare in Love* (1998): Joseph Fiennes plays a young William Shakespeare with writer's block. He's struggling with his new play (*Romeo and Ethel, the Sea Pirate's Daughter*) when the muse arrives in the form of Gwyneth Paltrow.

4. *Deconstructing Harry* (1997): Woody Allen plays Harry Block, a celebrated novelist who relies upon thinly veiled life experiences for his fiction.

5. *Throw Momma From The Train* (1987): Watch for great scenes with Billy Crystal as the director of a creative writing workshop.

Write from the point-of-view
of someone who committed
a murder today. Do not
mention the murder.

Goodbye

spark word

Urban Legends

Alligators in the sewers. The woman who paid $500 for a Neiman Marcus cookie recipe. The fashion model who was broiled alive after falling asleep in a suntanning booth. These are all urban legends—oddly compelling stories that are passed along by word of mouth and presented as the God's honest truth. The best of these legends feature surprise twist endings with all the punch of a good *Twilight Zone* episode (like the travelling salesman who went to a hotel with a mysterious woman . . . and woke up the next morning in a bathtub full of ice, realizing that one of his kidneys was

stolen by organ harvesters).

Take your favorite urban legend and use it as the inspiration for a sketch or short story. Write about gang members who lace ATM envelopes with LSD as an initiation ritual. Or the woman who stopped at a gas station and learned that an escaped ax murderer was crouched in the backseat of her car. Or the little boy in Idaho who will receive life-saving chemotherapy treatments if you forward an e-mail to twenty-five of your closest friends . . .

Write about
the first time
you defied
your parents.

Tell the story of how your
parents became engaged.

Begin in the Middle

Good stories hit the ground running—and you can accomplish this by "beginning in the middle." Consider the first sentence of Raymond Carver's "Elephant": "I knew it was a mistake to let my brother have the money." Or the opening line of Mario Puzo's *The Godfather*: "Amerigo Bonasera sat in New York Criminal Court Number three and waited for justice, vengeance on the men who had so cruelly hurt his daughter, who had tried to dishonor her." Or the beginning of Shirley Jackson's "Trial by Combat": "When Emily Johnson came home one evening to her furnished room and found

three of her handkerchiefs missing from the dresser drawer, she was sure who had taken them and what to do." All of these beginnings drop the reader squarely *in medias res*—in the middle of the action. They establish strained relationships, seething emotions, and buried suspicions; they also present questions that capture the reader's interest.

Write your own opening line that begins in the middle. Establish characters, situations, and conflicts with a few choice words. Then drop your readers right smack in the center.

Write about
your worst
habit.

Create a character
who is trying to
gain access to
a private club
or organization.

Speed Racers

Even a prolific novelist like Joyce Carol Oates comes off looking lazy compared to Georges Simenon, the French author who produced fifteen books of autobiography, one thousand short stories, and more than four hundred novels. Simenon often claimed to have written eighty pages before breakfast, and once wrote an entire book in just twenty-four hours. Other writers have worked at similar breakneck paces. Louisa May Alcott wrote *Little Women* in twenty-one days to rescue her family from debt; Anne Rice completed *Interview with the Vampire* in five weeks to meet a competition

deadline. And western writer Louis L'Amour wrote three novels a year for more than thirty years—over 115 books in all.

If you really want to test your abilities as a writer, plan a weekend in the next few months where you'll have forty-eight hours of solitary, uninterrupted writing time—take time off from work if you can, and rent a cheap hotel room if you can afford it. Unplug the TV and disconnect the phone. Set yourself an impossible goal and see how far you get.

Create a character who is
falsely accused of a crime.

Viagra®

Hone Your Eavesdropping Skills

You've probably been told since childhood that eavesdropping is impolite. But it's also one of the best ways to improve your skills with dialogue. By focusing on the speech patterns and rhythms of candid conversations, you'll gain a better understanding of how real people speak. Irish novelist Maeve Binchy (*Circle of Friends*) also advocates this approach, and goes so far as to recommend spying on people. "To get dialogue right, listen to everyone, everywhere," she wrote in an essay for *The Writer*. "Follow people so you can hear what they are saying.

To get a scene right for *Tara Road*, I spent two days watching mothers and teenage daughters buying clothes in a store. Never hang up on a crossed telephone line, watch people in planes and trains, and be vigilant the whole time."

Spend an hour at your local bus or train station, and make a conscious effort to overhear as many conversations as possible. Use one of them as the basis for your next scene or short story.

Update a classic fairy tale for readers in the 21st century. Cinderella in a sweat shop? Sleeping Beauty on Seconal? A rollerblading Rumpelstiltskin?

Indulgence

Richard Price grew up in a Bronx housing project and channeled his adolescent experiences into a great literary debut, *The Wanderers*, which he published at age twenty-four. Since then, he's written a number of excellent novels, including the meticulously researched *Clockers*, which chronicles the mid-80s crack epidemic with astonishing detail. Although Price is a research fanatic and admits to spending months collecting ideas for a novel, he encourages young writers to draw on their own experiences. During a teaching stint at Yale, Price gave his creative writing students the following assignment, which he described in an interview with *The Paris Review*: "I made

them all find a photograph of their family taken at least one year before the writer was born. I said, 'All right. Write me a story that starts the minute these people break this pose. Where did they go? What did they do?' We all have these stories about our family, most of them are apocryphal, but whether you love or hate your family, they're yours, and these are your stories."

Describe the most
inappropriate place you've
ever used as a restroom.

A Fresh Spin on Tired Clichés

For Dorothy Parker, selecting a name for her dog was just like choosing a name for a fictional character, and she consciously avoided anything that sounded too familiar. Her solution was one of the best dog names I've ever heard: Cliché!

Clichés are a common pitfall for many beginning writers, and the easiest way to avoid them is to read and read and read—as much as you can, fiction and biography and journalism and anything else you can get your hands on. By processing thousands of pages through your subconscious, you'll develop a "cliché radar"

that will zero in on phrases like "heart of gold" and "light as a feather." (Etymologists take note: the word *cliché* dates back to eighteenth century France and early newspaper publications; typesetters would keep commonly used phrases and expressions on easy-access blocks called clichés.)

Take a common cliché and write as though it were a literal truth. Describe a character who is "fat as a cow" or "skinny as a rail." Invent a fashion model who becomes "green with envy," or a cardiologist whose "heart swells with pride." Suspend left-brain impulses toward logic and common sense.

Write about a black sheep in your family. How did he or she become ostracized? And what are your personal feelings toward this person?

Tipsy

Coping With Criticism

Negative criticism can often lead to an extended case of writer's block—but if you want to write, you'll need a thick skin. Even the very best novelists deal with negative criticism all of their lives. Toni Morrison's *Tar Baby*, for example, was described by *The New Yorker* as "heavy-handed and ultimately unintelligible." William Burroughs' *Naked Lunch* was damned by the *New Republic* as "the merest trash . . . not worth a second look." And in their review of Raymond Carver's *What We Talk About When We Talk About Love*, the *Atlantic Monthly* declared, "There is nothing here to appease a

reader's basic literary needs." But Morrison, Burroughs, and Carver kept writing despite the negative reviews, and so should you.

In fact, you might channel the emotion you're feeling into a short story or character sketch. Write from the point-of-view of a savage book review editor, or a particularly abrasive member of a writing workshop. Have this person reveal something about themselves (unintentionally) in their critique. And next time someone slams your work, remember these words from T.S. Eliot: "The only critics worth reading are the critics who practice, and practice well, the art of which they write."

Take a character
from any of your
existing stories, and
describe what might
happen to him or
her in your vision
of the afterlife.

Hitchhiker

spark word

Lightning vs. Lightning Bug

Mark Twain dispensed plenty of advice to writers over his career, but perhaps no remark was more famous than this: "The difference between the right word and the nearly right word is the same as that between lightning and the lightning bug." Word choice is crucial in any story, and even the most arbitrary of decisions will establish and change the tone of your fiction. To illustrate this point, poet and novelist John Balaban asks his creative writing students to consider the words *stomach*, *belly*, *tummy*, *gut*, and *abdomen*. These words all refer

to the same thing, yet they all carry very different connotations (poets love to dwell on a pregnant mother's belly, but I've read very few odes to a pregnant mother's gut!). If you're having trouble with a story, review every line and make sure the tone is consistent. Have you written the word *love* when you really mean *affection*, *passion*, or *tenderness*? Are you using the word *money* when you mean *cash*, *currency*, *dough*, *capital*, or *moolah*? By fine-tuning word choice, you can zero in on the heart and soul of your fiction.

Write from the point-of-view of a woman who had an abortion today. Do not mention the abortion.

If You Like Piña Coladas . . .

The personal ad section of any newspaper is a fantastic resource for fiction writers; each listing is practically a character sketch in itself, describing everything from age and weight to interests, occupation, religion, and desires. So what are you waiting for? Pick up your local newspaper, choose an ad that intrigues you, and start writing from the point of view of its author. Never mind the boring "40 yo artist who enjoys conversation and walks on the beach." Instead, write about the "sexy 23 yo female ISO generous older gentle-

man." Or the "Rubenesque Beauty seeking friendly, funny Couch Potato." Or (if you really want to go out on a limb) the "married couple ISO female sex servant/slave for weekend fun in our beach house." As you write, concentrate on the attributes that writers might be unintentionally revealing about themselves (i.e. middle-aged men who feel compelled to mention their pilot's license, or women who end their ads with "NO LOSERS, NO CHEATS, NO HEAD GAMES!!!!").

Take any

exercise from

The Writer's Block

and write

it twice;

do one draft

in first person,

and another

in third person.

Oops

Take a Walk

Why do so many writers love to take walks? Austen, Blake, Carroll, Dickens, Emerson . . . one could easily keep moving through the alphabet, checking off the last names of writers who have chronicled their walks, strolls, hikes, and wanderings through urban cityscapes and pristine wilderness. The urge persists among contemporary writers, too. Sue Grafton walks three miles every morning before sitting down to write. And Joyce Carol Oates recommends using running as a way to destroy writer's block. In an essay on the subject for *The New York Times*, Oates explained,

"The runner who's a writer is running through the land and cityscapes of her fiction, like a ghost in a real setting." Regarding her own experiences, she said, "The structural problems I set for myself in writing, in a long, snarled, frustrating and sometimes despairing morning of work, for instance, I can usually unsnarl by running in the afternoon."

So there you have it—if you're feeling blocked, put on your sweatpants, limber up with a few stretches, and then set off through the landscapes of *your* fiction. If the mere threat of physical exercise is enough to suddenly end your writer's block, that's okay, too.

Concentrate on this inkblot for several minutes, then write about what you see.

Describe your most
embarrassing on-the-job
experience.

Lust

Blend Genres

It's hard to think of a more enduringly successful book than John Berendt's *Midnight in the Garden of Good and Evil*, which spent more than two hundred weeks (four years!) on *The New York Times* bestseller list. The success of the book was completely unexpected, in large part because it defied the convention of most bestsellers. As Berendt himself told *The Writer* magazine, "*Midnight* has no genre. It's not really a novel, but there are fictional techniques in it; it's not really a travel book, but there's travel in it; and it's not really a crime story, but there's a murder in it." By ignoring

the traditional rules and restrictions of any single genre, Berendt produced a book that all readers could enjoy.

Now take his success and learn from it. Write a scene or short story that deliberately blurs elements from two or more genres. Perhaps it's literary fiction in the form of a self-help manual (as in Lorrie Moore's knock-out collection, *Self-Help*). Or maybe you'll write a courtroom thriller about vampires, or a hard-boiled detective story that's set in the wild west. Choose an outrageous juxtaposition, then run with it.

Trace the journey of a five dollar bill through the lives of five different owners. What was exchanged during the transactions? How much (or how little) did the transaction mean to each of the people involved?

Going to Extremes

Personal obsessions are at the heart of many great novels—Vladimir Nabokov's *Lolita* comes to mind, as does John Fowles' *The Collector* and Ian McEwan's *Enduring Love*. But obsessions don't need to be criminal to be interesting, and there's no better proof of this than *The Guinness Book of World Records*, a fascinating annual document of extreme human behavior. Its pages feature thousands of capsule biographies about people like Angelica Unverhau, the owner of the world's largest collection of ballpoint pens (168,700 to date). Or Jennifer Murray, a fifty-seven-year-old

grandmother who was the first person to pilot a helicopter around the world. Or Arthur Blessitt, who has walked 33,151 miles through 277 nations while carrying an eight-foot-high wooden cross. Or Cindy Jackson, who dubs herself the "human Barbie doll" and has spent $99,600 on twenty-seven plastic surgery procedures. The entries go on and on, and it's often hard not to imagine fictional backgrounds for these people (how does someone end up with a ballpoint pen collection, anyway?). By beginning with a small shred of truth, you can free your imagination to generate utterly fantastic fiction.

Tell a story about "the one who got away." (That is, a person you might have had a romantic relationship with, if life circumstances had been different.)

In-laws

Read the Novels of Joan Collins

Why Joan Collins? The rationale is simple: if you read great contemporary authors like Umberto Eco or P.D. James, you're bound to feel intimidated. But if you read a lousy author like Joan Collins, you'll actually learn how *not* to write. Your local library should have at least one of Joan's first three novels: *Prime Time*, *Love and Desire and Hate*, and *Infamous*. Just flip open to any page and you're bound to find a howler like this one: "Her long fake *Laura's of La Cienega* fingernails were painted a particularly virulent shade of vermilion that

clashed with her overglossed cyclamen mouth." Or this one: "The steep stone steps crumbled like Camembert as she scrambled up them." Or this one: "She had curly carrot hair that reminded Barney of the strawberry milkshake he had sorely missed." I could go on and on and on, and I haven't even touched on the sex scenes (which include lines like "Damn it, woman, you do that like you're milking a cow."). Good grief!

Write about the physical
trait you would have
killed to change in
junior high school.

Fertility

Sheer Coincidence

You have unwittingly opened to the exact center of *The Writer's Block*. Given that there are 672 unnumbered pages in this book, the odds of landing on this spread are one in 336. So it's as good a place as any to observe that many good stories begin with chance or coincidence—about being the right person in the right place at the right time. A police officer walks past a gas station as a robbery unfolds. A beautiful woman is sitting at a soda fountain when a Hollywood casting agent stops in to use the pay phone. A corporate executive misses her flight because of heavy rush-hour

traffic—and later learns that the plane was hijacked by terrorists.

Novelist Paul Auster kept a list of coincidences in a red notebook and wrote about them in his nonfiction collection, *The Art of Hunger* (Auster's first novel, *City of Glass*, was inspired by a wrong number). Think back to the strangest coincidence in your life—the old high school pal you encountered while traveling through Egypt, or the chance encounter that led to your marriage—and write about it.

According to the
Florida Department
of Corrections,
more than one
hundred people
have registered on
a waiting list to
see an execution.

Write about one of them.

Describe a time when you pretended to be someone or something you're not.

Charles Frazier landed on the bestseller lists with his debut novel, *Cold Mountain*, a Civil War romance that was inspired by one of Frazier's distant ancestors. It's the story of a wounded Confederate soldier, Inman, who decides to abandon fighting and walk home to his pre-war sweetheart. More than seven years of writing (and fifteen drafts!) went into the writing of *Cold Mountain*, but the first seed of inspiration came from Frazier's great-great-grandfather, who passed along Inman's story to his children.

I interviewed Charles Frazier just two weeks before *Cold Mountain* won the National Book Award, and asked how much of the novel

was documented in his family history. Frazier replied, "There really wasn't much to be learned about this ancestor. Just an outline, but not a full story. At the time, I kept hoping I'd turn up some trove of information about this guy, and never did. Now, I think that it's really wonderful I didn't have more."

Describe a story that has been handed down through your family for generations, but resist the urge to do any formal research (at least until you have a first draft written). Instead, free yourself to imagine their lives.

Describe the biggest risk
you've ever taken.

Ladies Man

Write While You Sleep

Impossible, right? Of course. But some writers claim that sleep (and the subconscious mind) can be extremely successful in solving difficult problems in their fiction. Art Spiegelman explained it best in an interview with radio host Naomi Epel: "Often I'll find that if I go to sleep laying the day's problem out to myself, and get a fairly clear fix on the various strands and bits of what I was working on right before going to sleep, letting those be my last conscious thoughts, I'll more or less consistently wake up with the solution." This approach has also been advocated by authors like Sue

Grafton and Charles Johnson (who discovered an important plot element of *Middle Passage* in a dream).

If a particular element of your story is giving you trouble, concentrate on the problem—the characters, the situation, the setting—in the moments before you fall asleep. As Spiegelman said, let these be your "last conscious thoughts." And be sure to have a notebook handy for when you awaken the next morning.

Write a story that begins,

"The last time I saw my mother was fifteen years ago."

Vanity

Read the Newspaper

Truman Capote read through several different newspapers and magazines every day, and the habit ultimately rewarded him in spades. While leafing through *The New York Times* one day, a tiny article about a slain Kentucky farmer caught his eye. Capote caught the next plane to Wichita, and the seven-year creation of *In Cold Blood* began.

He's not the only writer to draw his inspiration from newspapers. Anne Tyler found the inspiration for *A Slipping Down Life* in a human interest story about a girl who'd slashed the name "Elvis" into her forehead

(Tyler's character attempts the same stunt, but uses a mirror as her guide, and winds up etching the name backwards). Elmore Leonard found his inspiration for Karen Cisco—and the novel *Out of Sight*—in a newspaper photograph of a female marshall holding a shotgun. "Just looking at the picture," he told one interviewer, "I thought, 'This is the next book.'"

Check today's local newspaper for a story that's *your* next book. Better yet, go to a large bookstore that offers newspapers from distant cities and countries, and discover an idea from around the globe.

Visit your local airport on a rainy day and find a flight that has been delayed. Stand near the ticket counter and wait for an argument to start. Record as many details as possible, then grab a chair and transcribe the experience as quickly as possible.

Anne Lamott is responsible for critically acclaimed novels like *Rosie* and *Crooked Little Heart*, but she's best known among writers for her best-selling *Bird by Bird*, a collection of essays about the writer's life. Within its pages, she cautions her students not to have false illusions about getting their work in print: "Publication is not going to change your life or solve your problems. Publication will not make you more confident or more beautiful, and it will probably not make you any richer. There will be a very long buildup to publication day, and then the festivities will usually be over rather quickly."

If you constantly indulge fantasies of fame

upon publication, then consider the obvious and write about these fantasies. Put your acceptance speech for the Pulitzer Prize on paper. Transcribe your interview with Charlie Rose or Oprah Winfrey. These exercises may feel silly or self-indulgent, but whatever emotions you tap will certainly be genuine. And as you create this autobiographical future, you may find yourself on an unexpected fictional tangent.

Write about your partner's first sexual experience.

Write a story that begins,

"Three days passed before they found the body."

Take Comfort in Revision

Sometimes writer's block is the result of fear. I recently spoke with Melissa Jacobs, an Editor for St. Martin's Press, who told me that one of her projects was nearly two years past deadline. And to make matters worse, the author was barely halfway through the manuscript! What could account for such tardiness? Melissa's explanation was simple: "This subject matter is very personal and close to the author's heart. And as long as she doesn't write the story, she can still write the perfect story."

We all have great stories inside our minds. But the true challenge of writing is channeling

these stories into words and sentences and paragraphs. You may feel an enormous pressure to get the story exactly right. But you would do well to remember the advice of Ernest Hemingway, who said, "The first draft is always shit." Melissa offers similar counsel to her authors (although she phrases it more delicately): "Take comfort in revision," she tells them. "Every writer does revisions. So why worry about getting it right the first time when you have to revise it, anyway?"

Write about the
worst driving
you've ever done.

Debt

spark word

Isabel Allende was born in Chile and worked as a journalist in South America until January 8, 1981, when she received a phone call that her beloved grandfather was dying. She immediately began composing a letter to him, and it evolved into her first novel, *The House of the Spirits.* Since then, Allende has written many more books (including *Of Love and Shadows*, *Aphrodite*, and *Paula*, a memoir about the life and loss of her daughter), but she always begins a new book on January 8. "[It's] a sacred day for me," Allende explains on her personal website (www.isabelallende.com). "I come to my office very early in the morning, alone. I light some candles for the spirits and

the muses. I meditate for a while. I always have fresh flowers and incense. And I open myself completely to this experience that begins in that moment." Think of a date that is especially notable to yourself—perhaps it's the day you met a loved one, the day you quit a dead-end job, or simply a day you found twenty dollars on the sidewalk. Use the exact calendar date as your title and write a story about it.

Describe the first person who broke your heart. If you had the chance to take revenge on them, would you?

Tabloid Trash

They're the newspapers you see in the checkout line of your local supermarket, with screaming 48-point headlines like "BAT CHILD FOUND IN CAVE!" and "I GOT PREGNANT DURING A COMPUTER SEX CHAT!" Most people dismiss these stories as tabloid trash, but a few imaginative artists have recognized them as a rich source of inspiration. In 1980, David Byrne wrote and directed his first motion picture, *True Stories*, which was based on these "real-life" news features. More recently, Pulitzer Prize winner Robert Olen Butler wrote *Tabloid Dreams*, a col-

lection of loosely related short stories with titles like "Titanic Victim Speaks Through Waterbed" and "Woman Uses Glass Eye to Spy on Philandering Husband."

Next time you're waiting in line at the supermarket, pick up the *Weekly World News* and see if any of the stories spark your imagination. If you want to begin immediately, use any of these headlines as a jumping-off point:

MIRACLE CAT READS THE BIBLE!
ST. LOUIS WOMAN LAYS GIANT EGGS!
I WAS SEXUALLY MOLESTED BY A
    FEMALE BIGFOOT!
MINK COAT COMES ALIVE AND BITES
    RICH WIDOW TO DEATH!

Thirty-four percent of new American public school teachers say they plan to quit their profession within five years.

Write about one of them.

Bird

A Good Title is Hard to Find

It's amazing how many good books start out with bad titles. Would you ever pick up novels called *Pansy, Before This Anger,* or *Something That Happened*? Probably not. Yet these were the working titles for *Gone with the Wind, Roots,* and *Of Mice and Men*. Good titles are hard to come by, and writers look for them everywhere—in the Bible (*Absalom, Absalom!, East of Eden, Stranger in a Strange Land*), in the works of Shakespeare (*Brave New World, Remembrance of Things Past, Something Wicked This Way Comes*), and, more recently, in the

lyrics of popular music (the past few years have seen novels called *Brown-Eyed Girl*, *American Pie*, and even *Girlfriend in a Coma*).

F. Scott Fitzgerald kept a special notebook just for writing down titles, and you might do the same. Pull ideas from every possible source: TV, movies, radio jingles, fortune cookies, computer error messages, restaurant menus, everywhere. Then choose the title that intrigues you the most, and write a story to go with it.

Write about an incident that could be used against you if you ever ran for political office.

Ouch

Scott Turow is responsible for some of the most well-written legal thrillers in bookstores today, including best-selling novels like *Presumed Innocent* and *The Laws of Our Fathers*. Perhaps to stay on top of his subject matter, Turow maintains his job as a full partner at his law firm. But how, you might ask, does someone *without* a law degree prepare to write a legal thriller? Turow's official website (www.scottturow.com) features a top-ten list of law-related books that any writer of courtroom thrillers would benefit from. Presented in no particular ranking, they are: *Billy Budd* by Herman Melville, *To Kill a Mockingbird* by Harper Lee, *The Just and the Unjust* by

James Gould Cozzens, *A Theory of Justice* by John Rawls, *The Rumpole Stories* by John Mortimer, *Snow Falling on Cedars* by David Guterson, *A Married Man* by Piers Paul Read, *The Trial and Death of Socrates* by Plato, *Bleak House* by Charles Dickens, and *The Merchant of Venice* by William Shakespeare.

Invent a character who must choose between the lesser of two evils.

Desire

One of the quickest ways to grab a reader is to make your characters want something. Louisa May Alcott's *Little Women* opens with Jo grumbling the now-famous line, "Christmas won't be Christmas without any presents." Ira Levin's *Rosemary's Baby* begins with Guy and Rosemary Woodhouse trying to find an affordable apartment in Manhattan. And John Steinbeck's *The Pearl* opens with Kino seeking a doctor for his son.

These desires, although commonplace, lead to extraordinary sequences of events. When Kurt Vonnegut taught creative writing, he

encouraged students to make their characters want something right away. In an interview with *The Paris Review*, he recalled, "One of my students wrote a story about a nun who got a piece of dental floss stuck between her lower left molars, and who couldn't get it out all day long. I thought that was wonderful. The story dealt with issues a lot more important than dental floss, but what kept readers going was anxiety about when the dental floss would finally be removed."

Begin a story in which a character wants something—a loan, a parking space, a glass of water, anything—right away.

Write a love story set in cyberspace.

Have the story consist entirely of alternating chat lines.

Describe a time when you've settled an argument between two close friends.

Panic

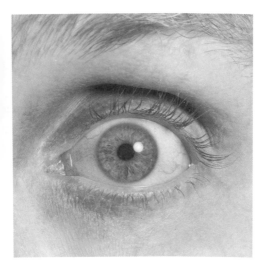

Three Lousy Movies About Writer's Block

Rent 'em and think to yourself: "I know I can write better than this!"

1. *Skin Deep* (1989): John Ritter plays an alcoholic writer who cannot muster the inspiration to complete his latest novel. The trailers for this movie relied heavily on its only good joke, which concerns a pitch-dark bedroom and some glow-in-the-dark condoms. 'Nuff said.

2. *Move* (1979): Elliott Gould is a playwright who overcomes writer's block by writing pornography, and later gets to live out the fantasies of his fiction. The perfect movie for any-

one who's ever said, "Boy, I'd love to watch Elliott Gould live out some pornographic fantasies."

3. *Her Alibi* (1989): How bad is bad? Over the course of this romantic comedy, the novelist played by Tom Selleck is beaten up by a guy in a clown suit, shot in the ass with an arrow, and squirted in the face with windshield wiper fluid. His co-star, Paulina Porizkova, plays a Romanian immigrant with lines like, "I do not fit in your world," and "Can you not feel the twin points of my two love globes crushed against your chest?"

Write about a library or bookstore that has special significance to you. Which authors did you discover there?

Conformity

Toni Morrison enjoys a critical and commercial success that very few writers can match (after all, how many other Nobel Prize winners have also appeared on Oprah Winfrey's Book Club?). Along with writers Russell Banks and E.L. Doctorow, she makes her home in Princeton, New Jersey, and teaches an extremely popular writing class at Princeton University. Most students would give their right arm to enroll in it, but here's a free tip that Morrison dispensed in an interview with *The Paris Review*: "I tell my students one of the most important things they need to know is when they are their best, creatively. They need to ask themselves, What does the

ideal room look like? Is there music? Is there silence? Is there chaos outside or is there serenity outside? What do I need in order to release my imagination?" If you suffer from writer's block, ask these questions to yourself: Where do you write well? During what time of day are you most creative? Then adjust your surroundings in a way that best suits your imagination.

Invent a character
whose life is governed by
Murphy's Law (that is,
anything that *can*
go wrong *will*).

Wish

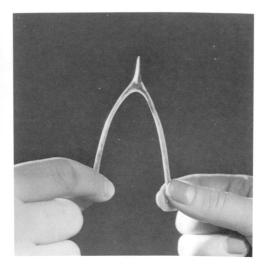

Push Yourself

How many pages do you write a day? Ernest Hemingway believed that "wearing down seven number two pencils is a good day's work." Paul Auster, on the other hand, prefers to "inch along" and feels satisfied if he produces one "pretty good" page. Crime writer Elmore Leonard has a daily quota of six to eight pages, and Tom Wolfe strives for ten: "[W]hat I write when I force myself is generally just as good as what I write when I'm feeling inspired. It's mainly a matter of forcing yourself to write."

So force yourself to write. Start typing and

don't stop until you've hit 2,500 words (a typed double-spaced page usually averages 250). Don't edit yourself as you go along—the finished piece doesn't have to make sense. The goal here is quantity, not quality. Allow your mind to wander; encourage strange leaps of the imagination. By forcing your imagination to produce—and by pushing yourself beyond your usual limits—your subconscious may yield wonderful surprises.

Write a story that begins with
a phone call at three o'clock
in the morning.

Write it Down

F. Scott Fitzgerald was obsessive about keeping notebooks, and the best of this material was collected by Edmund Wilson in a fascinating volume called *The Crack-Up*. Fitzgerald organized his notebooks in a unique alphabetical format: Section A was full of anecdotes, Section C recounted conversations overheard, Section G listed descriptions of girls, and so on; Fitzgerald also kept separate notebooks for titles, observations, even jingles and songs. He clearly understood what many writers learn the hard way: "flashes of inspiration" usually vanish if you don't write them down.

For this very reason, Joseph Heller walked around with a packet of index cards in his wallet, and was constantly jotting down sentences. Anne Lamott never leaves a house without an index card, either. "I might be walking along the salt marsh, or out at Phoenix Lake, or in the express line at Safeway, and suddenly I hear something wonderful that makes me want to smile or snap my fingers . . . and I take out my index card and scribble it down." Get in the habit of carrying your own index cards, and never trust a great observation to memory.

Write about the

worst lie

someone told you.

Why did they lie?

How did you find out,

and how did your

discovery change your

relationship?

911

Writing for the Screen

If you're stuck in a work of fiction, try re-writing your story in the form of a screenplay. By stripping the narrative down to its most basic elements—dialogue and action—you may discover things about the story you hadn't realized. And plenty of good writers before you have dabbled in the form, to varying degrees of success: Dorothy Parker wrote everything from a silly Bing Crosby film (*Here is My Heart*) to an Alfred Hitchcock thriller (*Saboteur*). Martin Amis received critical acclaim for novels like *Time's Arrow* and *London Fields*, but he also penned the screen-

play to the 1980 Farrah Fawcett film *Saturn 3* (which was panned by Roger Ebert as "awesomely stupid, totally implausible from a scientific viewpoint, and a shameful waste of money.") And Rita Mae Brown—now famous for writing mysteries about her cat—also wrote the script for *Slumber Party Massacre*, a campy '80s horror flick. For information on the proper formatting of screenplays, just pay a visit to the Internet, where hundreds of Hollywood scripts are available free to would-be screenwriters.

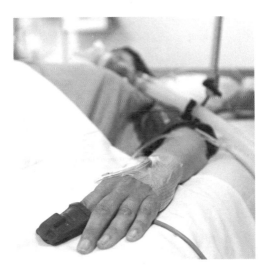

Write from the
point of view of a
character on his or
her deathbed.

Polygamy

Joyce Carol Oates is one of the most prolific contemporary authors writing today, with more than thirty-five novels, eight volumes of poetry, and four hundred short stories to her credit. So what's her secret? Aside from a rigorous twelve-hour work schedule, Oates also has an unusual writing/editing/revision process, which she described in a conversation with *The Paris Review*: "When I complete a novel I set it aside, and begin work on short stories, and eventually another long work. When I complete that novel I return to the earlier novel and rewrite much of it. In the meantime the second novel lies in a desk drawer. Sometimes I work on two

novels simultaneously, though one usually forces the other into the background."

Developing two or three projects simultaneously is good "preventative maintenance" against writer's block; if you find yourself stuck or losing interest in one story, you can simply jump to another. The important thing is to keep writing, to keep developing your skills—and if your output is just a fraction of Joyce Carol Oates', you'll be in pretty good shape.

Write about your favorite childhood toy.

Write Naked

When you sit down to write every day, what are you wearing? Corporations have found that dress codes have a direct result on the attitudes and productivity of their employees (hence the trend toward "business casual" in recent years) And if clothing can affect major corporations, you better believe it's affecting your writing. James Michener liked to dress in baggy Bermuda shorts, oversized t-shirts, and floppy sandals; he once observed, "I have grown to feel wonderfully at ease in that uniform; it restricts me at no point and leaves my arms and hands free to move easily." Sue

Grafton, on the other hand, arrives at her desk in a fresh-pressed business suit ("I don't work in my jammies," she told one reporter. "This is a professional job.") The French novelist Victor Hugo fell somewhere between these extremes—he often wrote in the nude.

Next time you sit down to write, alter your typical routine and try dressing up—à la Sue Grafton—or dressing down, like James Michener. (You may also try the Victor Hugo approach, but be sure you close the blinds first!)

Write about a character who
is granted three wishes.

Deadline

The Importance of Avoiding Adverbs

When I was seventeen, I wrote an awful short story called "Prom Night." Why was it bad? For starters, the story had more to do with proms I'd seen on TV than proms I'd attended in real life. But an even bigger problem was the story's dependence on clunky -ly adverbs; in just seven pages, I'd managed to use more than fifty. Consider this (mercifully brief) exchange between my prom dates, Glenn and Tina:

They stood under the awning, holding each other tightly.

"So what now?" Glenn asked questioningly.

Tina licked her lips. "Want to come upstairs?" she asked seductively.

Three rules I have learned since then: Never use the word "tightly" to modify the word "holding." Never use the word "questioningly" after the verb "asked." And never use the adverb "seductively" in a sentence where a woman licks her lips. All of these adverbs are restating the obvious—you can cut them without changing the meaning of the sentences.

Flip to any Writing Challenge or Spark Word in *The Writer's Block*, and complete the exercise without using any adverbs or adjectives. Focus on selecting the strongest nouns and verbs at your disposal.

Write about a victim of "year-end fiscal cutbacks and corporate downsizing."

Write about a wedding during
which the bride or groom
changes their mind.

Your Fictional Universe

Some writers return to the same setting again and again, and wind up creating a vast, fully realized fictional universe. Perhaps the best example is William Faulkner, whose Yuknapatowpha County was the setting for more than a dozen novels and plenty of short stories; important families, characters, and major historical events are cross-referenced throughout. Thomas Hardy accomplished a similar feat with his novels, which were set in the fictional county of Wessex. Louise Erdrich's novels take place in the fictional town of Argus, North Dakota, and Roddy

Doyle's first four novels were set in the imaginary community of Barrytown. Some fantasy and science fiction writers go even further, creating new languages, cultures, and species for their worlds.

Look back at an old story that you're especially proud of, and choose a minor character who makes a fleeting appearance—a cab driver, perhaps, or a supermarket grocer. Tell an all-new story from this person's point of view. Continue building your own fictional world, one character at a time.

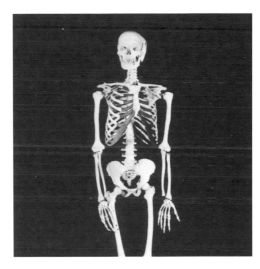

Describe the skeletons
in your family's closets.

Discipline

Anne Tyler is responsible for such exquisitely structured novels as *Breathing Lessons*, *The Accidental Tourist*, and *A Patchwork Planet*, but very few of her admirers would believe that her novels begin in such a haphazard fashion. During an interview with *The New York Times*, Tyler explained that she used up hundreds of index cards for scribbling down ideas—sometimes just the smallest shreds of an idea, like a conversation she'd heard on a bus or a line like, "Around the house, Cobb wears kneesocks with her housedress." These cards are filed in a meticulously organized set of boxes, which Tyler reviews during the early stage of a new novel. "At every fifth card or so

a little click will go in my mind and I think, 'Boy that would be fun,' and I start to expand on it . . . . At the end I have maybe ten cards, and they are such disparate things that the problem is how on earth am I going to get them all into one framework?"

Try using Tyler's system for your own fiction. Aim to write down ten ideas over the course of a single day—and then write a story that incorporates all of these elements.

Tell a story in
the form of a
love letter.

This is a Work of Fiction

Beginning in the 1940s and '50s, most novels began to feature a disclaimer like this one on their copyright pages: "This is a work of fiction, and therefore all names, characters, places, and incidents are products of the author's imagination. Any resemblance to actual events, locales, or persons, living or dead, is entirely coincidental."

Entirely coincidental? Hardly! Novelists are always looking to actual events, locales, and persons for their inspiration—it's their job. So I'm glad to see that many publishers are dropping this disclaimer from their books. And

the copyright page of Dave Eggers' *A Heartbreaking Work of Staggering Genius* actually parodies the convention: "This is a work of fiction, only in that in many cases, the author could not remember the exact words said by certain people, and exact descriptions of certain things, so he had to fill in gaps as best he could."

If you're stuck in the middle of a story, try writing a disclaimer that prefaces it. Perhaps you should publicly acknowledge all of the family members whose identities are barely concealed. Or apologize to your ex for spilling the beans about your lousy sex life.

Research an unsolved
murder that occurred
in your city or town.

Speculate about
what might have
really happened.

Loser

Magic Tunes

I used to think I was unique in choosing "soundtracks" for my characters—certain CDs or songs that I would play over and over while working on a particular chapter or short story. But I've since learned that writers have been using this approach for years. Anne Sexton wrote a great deal of her poetry while listening to "Bachianas Brasileiras" by Villa-Lobos (she told *The Paris Review*, "it's my magic tune.") Dorothy Allison used gospel music to help write *Bastard Out of Carolina*, but switched to rock and roll for her next novel, *Cavedweller*. (She told one interviewer, "I use

music to pin down my characters in my own mind, playing the same records over and over as I work.") Nick Hornby also uses rock for inspiration; during the writing of his second novel, *About a Boy*, he kept plenty of Nirvana and REM in his CD player.

What are your magic tunes? What song or album best reflects the personalities of your characters, or the mood of your story? If you're not sure, go to a music store with "listening stations" and find one that does.

Tell a story that centers around a recipe.

Describe your first
encounter with
a celebrity.

Tell the story twice—
first from your
point of view,
then imagine how
the celebrity felt
about meeting you.

Outcast

Fear of Fear Itself

Forcing your characters to confront their fears is an effective way to generate conflict. A character with *dentophobia* (fear of dentists) might choose between weeks of excruciating pain or a two-hour root canal. An account executive with severe *aviophobia* (fear of flying) might have to choose between a coast-to-coast flight or losing a big client. The motivation explaining *why* a character confronts fear may be more interesting than the source of the fear itself. With this in mind, write about any of these phobias, all of which have been documented in medical journals: *lockiophobia* (fear

of childbirth), *lygophobia* (fear of the dark), *ophidiophobia* (fear of snakes), *phalacrophobia* (fear of becoming bald), *triskaidekaphobia* (fear of the number 13), *venustraphobia* (fear of beautiful women), *pupaphobia* (fear of puppets), *misophobia* (fear of contamination), the surprisingly common *gephyrophobia* (fear of crossing bridges), and, of course, *phobophobia* (fear of fear itself).

According to a poll conducted by the Gallup Organization, 10% of Americans say they have communicated with the devil. Write a story about one of these encounters.

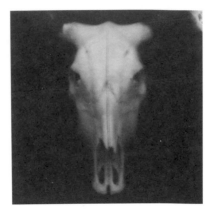

Seduction

Take Up a Hobby

Another way to lend a three-dimensional quality to your characters is to give them a hobby. Detective Nero Wolfe spent his time between mysteries growing orchids. The record store clerks in Nick Hornby's *High Fidelity* are obsessed with pop music. One of the most famous lines from *The Silence of the Lambs* concerns Hannibal Lecter's fondness for Chianti; his appreciation of wine and fine art made him a fully realized character in a genre that's full of stereotypes. (Norman Bates never drank a Chianti in his life, but it's worth remembering that *his* hobby was taxidermy.)

Sometimes a hobby will reveal insights into the personality of a character. Detective Philip Marlow devoted much of his leisure time to playing chess—against himself. And at the end of Lawrence Block's *Hit Man*, the titular character realizes he has more than enough money to retire—then begins collecting expensive stamps as an excuse to justify staying in his profession.

If you're blocked in the middle of a story, look at your characters and reflect on their hobbies. How do they spend their free time? Why do they choose to spend it this way? And what does it say about them?

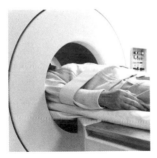

Write about the most serious injury
or health problem you've ever faced.

Make a Commitment

Lots of writers have an unfinished novel collecting dust in the space underneath their beds. But I've known some writers who seem to *specialize* in unfinished novels. They get a flash of inspiration, begin a few chapters, sketch out some characters, and work for a few months, but then ultimately discard the project to pursue another newer, fresher flash of inspiration. Needless to say, this pattern has been known to repeat itself.

Stephen King summed up the process with an excellent analogy: "Working on a new idea is kind of like getting married. Then a new

idea comes along and you think, 'Man, I'd really like to go out with her.' But you can't. At least not until the old idea is finished . . . ." Be faithful to your projects. If you've invested several months in a novel, you owe it to yourself to pull through the bad periods, to try your hardest to make the material work. Take a rest if you want, but leave the manuscript in plain sight, on top of your desk. Yes, there are some times when a writer should call it quits. But don't go down without a fight.

Invent a character who sees a
phone number on a restroom
wall. Describe what happens
when he or she dials it.

Unpopular

spark word

Ethan Canin enrolled in the Iowa Writer's Workshop at the age of twenty-two— and felt so "utterly paralyzed" by the experience that he barely completed two short stories in two years. After finishing the program, he enrolled in Harvard Medical School, where the stories began pouring out of him. While dealing with the brutal workloads that cause many medical students to drop out, Canin completed the ten stories in his first book, *Emperor of the Air*, which won a Houghton Mifflin Literary Fellowship. That success was followed by two novels, *Blue River* and *For Kings and Planets*, as well as a book of novellas, *The Palace Thief*. "I've always set assignments

for myself," Canin told *The Atlantic Monthly*. "The assignment for the story 'Emperor of the Air,' for example, was to write a story in which an unlikable character becomes likable by the end. For 'Accountant,' it was to write a story in which a pair of socks takes on large emotional importance."

If you're not familiar with either of these stories, you might tackle one of these assignments yourself—then read Canin's work and see how he met the challenge.

Invent the Perfect Crime.

Describe the most meaningful and/or important gift you've ever received. What does it reveal about your relationship to the giver?

What Book Influences Your Writing the Most?

On many occasions, John Irving has told interviewers, "*Great Expectations* is the first novel I read that made me wish I had written it; it is the novel that made me want to be a novelist—specifically, to move a reader as I was moved then." Nearly every writer has books that he or she holds close to their heart. Madison Smartt Bell estimates that, as a young man, he must have read *All the King's Men* once a year for ten years straight. Harry Crews reads *Madame Bovary* every year, sometimes twice a year. And writers ranging from Anna

Quindlen and Amy Bloom to Cynthia Ozick list *Pride and Prejudice* as one of the most influential novels in their lives.

If you had to name any one novel that made you want to be a writer, what would it be? And when was the last time you read it? By reconnecting with a novel that inspired you to write, you may find the spark of inspiration you're looking for.

Describe your most intimate experience with Mother Nature.

Valentine's Day

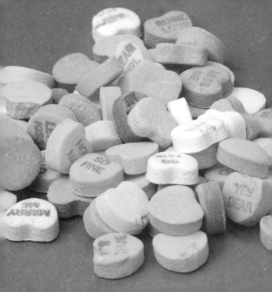

Write Everywhere

If there's one thing journalists know about fiction writing, it's this: You can write anywhere, anytime, as long as you have a pad and pencil. In fact, sometimes a new environment can provide an unexpected burst of inspiration. Neil Simon writes everywhere he can, even in the dentist's office. Richard Ford wrote his novella "The Womanizer" on a flight from Paris to the United States (but if you can't afford an international flight ticket, you can try writing on the bus, which often worked for Joseph Heller). Scott Turow spent eight years writing *Presumed Innocent* on the morning

commuter train. Bookstore cafes and coffee shops are also popular with writers, and I'm partial to the dining areas of fast food restaurants like McDonalds and Burger King (they're less trendy than Starbucks, but tend to attract some very eccentric personalities). Finally, of course, there are always libraries (where a young, impoverished Ray Bradbury composed *Fahrenheit 451*, using typewriters that charged ten cents for thirty minutes of typing time). If the environment of a good library doesn't inspire you to write *anything*, you may need more help than this book can offer!

Invent a character who suspects his or her spouse of infidelity. Perhaps the story starts with a mysterious phone call, or the discovery of unfamiliar shoes beneath the bed . . .

a "nonfiction novel" about a murder in Savannah.

Of course, you don't need to travel to the big city to utilize Wolfe's approach—a short car trip of fifty miles will bring nearly anyone to a small town that's full of history, mystery, bizarre customs, and lore. Step outside your world and write about what you find.

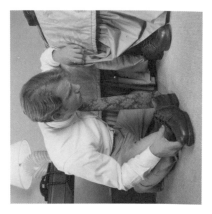

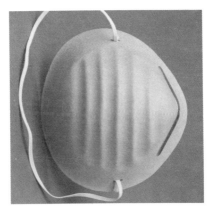

Describe the secret life
of a school bus driver.

More than 25,000
Americans seek help
every year for
compulsive gambling.

Write about one of them.

Revisit the Classics

In recent years, many novelists have taken a classic work of literature and re-told the story from a secondary character's point-of-view. Some examples you may know are Elizabeth Cooke's *Zeena* (a re-telling of *Ethan Frome* from the point of view of his wife), Gregory Maguire's *Wicked* (in which the Wicked Witch of the West gets to tell her side of the story), Sena J. Naslund's *Ahab's Wife* (concerning the famous whale hunter of *Moby Dick*), John Gardner's *Grendel* (which is about the monster from the epic poem *Beowulf*), and Jean Rhys' *Wide Sargasso Sea*, which describes the

mysterious "Mad Woman in the Attic" from Charlotte Brontë's *Jane Eyre*.

Think back to your favorite classics, and to secondary characters whose stories were left untold. What does Jim really think of Huck Finn, anyway? What would a therapist's analysis of Holden Caulfield sound like? Don't be shy, and don't worry about what your old English professors might say—no classic is too sacred if it gets your ideas flowing.

Write about your first kiss.

Describe your most memorable family holiday, and explain what made it special for you.

Brand Recognition

When your narrator goes for a run, does he reach for his sneakers or lace up his *Nikes*? When his wife gets home, does she pour herself a beer or reach for an ice-cold *Corona*? Over the last twenty years, many writers have capitalized on the immediacy that brand names bring to fiction, and perhaps no one does this better than Stephen King. Ever wonder how he pulled off "Apt Pupil," a completely believable novella about a deranged ex-Nazi who kills with the assistance of his 13-year-old paperboy? Part of its effectiveness comes from mentioning dozens of brand names, so readers

recognize the story's world as their own (a *New York Times* reviewer found references to Nike, Timex, Schwinn, I.B.M., HBO, Hush Puppies, Budweiser, Reader's Digest, Kodak, Kools, National Geographic, A-1 Steak Sauce, Scotch Tape, Ring Dings, Hall's Mentholyptus, Motorola, Hyatt, Porsche, Coke, Krazy Glue, "The Flintstones," Shell No-Pest Strips, Big Macs, Revlon, Diamond Blue-Tip matches, Lawn-Boy, and Wildroot Cream Oil).

Pick up a magazine, leaf through the advertisements, and write a short piece that mentions any three of the products advertised. What do your choices reveal about your characters?

Bad Hair Day

spark word

Try to reveal the
source of the
narrator's misguided
beliefs within the
monologue, and make
the reader ultimately
sympathize with
the speaker.

According to the Gallup
Organization, more than
one million American dogs
have been named as
beneficiaries in a will.

Write about one of
their owners.

Marge Piercy has established a reputation as both a novelist (*Three Women, Fly Away Home* and *Gone to Sailors*) and a poet (*The Art of Blessing the Day, Mars and Her Children*). In an essay for *The New York Times*, Piercy explained the benefits of wearing two hats: "Sometimes I say that if a writer works in more than one genre, the chances of getting writer's block are greatly diminished. If I am stuck in a difficult passage of a novel, I may jump ahead to smoother ground, or I may pause and work on poems exclusively for a time. If I lack ideas for one genre, usually I have them simmering for the other." Piercy is not alone in this regard; the list of novel-

ists/poets includes Margaret Atwood, John Updike, Erica Jong, and Alice Walker.

If you're stuck in the middle of a story or novel, try writing a poem about the aspect that is troubling you. Maybe it's a particular character's motivation—or lack thereof. By addressing the question in a different genre, you may push through to a solution.

Imagine a use for the machine in this photograph. Then tell a story from the point of view of the machine repair person.

Prodigy

The Myth of the Muse

As an editor, I meet plenty of people who tell me they have novels "in their heads," that they're simply waiting for "the muse to strike." And of course these people never ever *ever* write books, because real writers don't have muses—real writers usually write every day whether they feel like it or not. As the author of more than twenty-three best-selling thrillers, Mary Higgins Clark understands this better than anyone. In an interview with the website Writers Write, Clark said, "So many people tell me, 'I'm going to write a book as soon as. . . .' The three fatal words are *as soon a*

As soon as I quit my job. As soon as the kids grow up. As soon as the dog dies. But trust me, as soon as the kids grow up and the dog dies, there will be a new set of excuses not to write which will be equally valid." So stop waiting for your muse and just write. If it helps you get started, write a scene where you confront your would-be muse in person. What does he or she look like? And where the hell have they been? ·

Write about your earliest
childhood memory.

Clueless

The Sincerest Form
of Flattery

Who are your influences? What writers make you want to write? If you could have written any of the novels at your local Barnes & Noble, which one would it be? Chances are, you're already imitating its author—and that's not a bad thing. Writers learn from imitation, from mixing and melding styles until we've reached a fully formed voice to call our own. One way to speed the process along is to *consciously* imitate someone, by deliberately writing in the short, clipped sentences of Ernest Hemingway, or the flat, deadpan tone of a Raymond

Chandler narrator. You can begin writing from scratch, or you can follow the advice of celebrated creative writing teachers Anne Bernays and Pamela Painter, who advise their students to review their favorite short stories and "find a place between two sentences that seem like a 'crack' that could be 'opened up.'" Next, expand the paragraph while remaining true to the original author's style, tone, plot, and characterization. You probably won't improve on the original work, but you'll learn a great deal about what makes it work!

There are approximately 3,500 members in the International Flat Earth Society (people who insist that the Earth is not round). Write about one of them.

Bachelor

spark word

Sue Grafton turned to mystery writing as a way to escape her life as a screenwriter, which she detested ("I don't like to write by committee," she has said, "[and] I don't like to sit in a room with twenty-six-year-olds telling me how to do my job.") Thus Kinsey Millhone and the famous "alphabet mystery series" were born: *A is for Alibi, B is for Burglar, C is for Corpse*, et al. Grafton is also one of the rare authors who claim to "love" writer's block, and advises young authors to consider it a tool: "Instead of looking at writer's block as a terrible thing that you have to thrash and bash yourself out of or power through, it's much better to get quiet and look

at what that message from your psyche actually is." In other words: If you're stuck in a story, there's a reason you're stuck. Try to look at the work objectively. Ignore your ego and listen to your subconscious.

Write a "locked room" mystery. (In a traditional locked room mystery, a dead body is discovered alone in a room that has been locked from the inside.)

Voyeur

Talking Down

To most people, writing for children looks easy—fewer pages and fewer words equals less work, right? In fact, the market for children's books is fiercely competitive, with tens of thousands of manuscripts being rejected every year. So what's the most common mistake made by first time authors? I asked that question to children's book editor Patty Smith, who has worked with award-winning writers like Shel Silverstein. "A lot of beginners get bogged down with morals," Smith told me. "A moral should never be driving a story. And a moral should never be confused with a plot." In other

words, it's okay to have a lesson, but don't let the lesson interfere with your telling of a good tale. "You can't preach to kids," Smith adds, "and you can't talk down to them, either. It's amazing how they sense condescension."

To fully understand the dangers of "preachy" fiction, write a page or two by a narrator who is extremely condescending. Exaggerate his or her ego to the point where it becomes comical. Have them labor to make a point that is ridiculously obvious or trivial.

Write about the most important event or meeting that you've ever been late to.

Strike

Unreliable Narrators

It takes an exceptional writer to create a narrator who is unreliable and yet nevertheless compelling. Consider young, naïve Huck Finn, who describes (but doesn't always comprehend) what he witnesses on the Mississippi River. Or the young governess in Henry James' *The Turn of the Screw*, whose journal entries leave much of what already happened open to debate. And then there is Charles Kinbote, the dishonest narrator of Vladimir Nabokov's *Pale Fire*. In describing his admiration for the poet John Shade, Kinbote reveals his capacity for self-delusion with lines like,

"And he was a very dear friend indeed! The calendar says I had known him only for a few months but there exist friendships which develop their inner duration, their own eons of transparent time. . . ."

Write a few pages from the point of view of an unreliable narrator. This person may be consciously or unconsciously providing misinformation to the reader. Aim to create a story that provides two different kinds of information—what the narrator is deliberately telling us, and what the narrator is unintentionally telling us.

Tell the story behind your nickname,

or the story of the most unusual
nickname you've ever heard.

Temptation

Love Stories

There's big money in writing tearjerkers, according to the Romance Writers of America (RWA). Their website (www.rwanational.com) states that romance fiction comprises 38.8% of all contemporary fiction sold (compared to 25.7% for mystery/suspense fiction and 7.3% for science fiction/fantasy), making it the most popular genre in today's fiction market. So what are some guidelines for the first-time author? The RWA states that "Two basic elements comprise every romance novel: a central love story and an emotionally satisfying and optimistic ending." Beyond these simple con-

straints, however, there's a wide range of sub-genres to explore: Contemporary, Historical, Inspirational (containing Judeo-Christian themes), Paranormal (with magic or other fantastic elements), Regency (set in England in the early 1800s), Suspense, and Time-travel (in which characters from two different time periods interact).

With more than two thousand romances being published every year, you won't find a genre that's more friendly to unpublished authors. So why not pick a sub-genre and see how you like it?

Write about
your greatest
childhood fear.

Gossip

Don't Get Mad—Get Even

Shirley Jackson admitted that her first novel, *The Road Through the Wall*, was written mainly to "get back at" her parents, and she's not the only author who has used revenge as a motivation. William Gass once observed, "I write because I hate. A lot. Hard." And Andrei Codrescu says he writes to get back at all the people who harassed him while growing up.

Write about a person you do not like—perhaps it's your boss or your ex-spouse or your next-door neighbor. Maybe, like Shirley Jackson, you have unresolved issues with your parents. Plumb the depths of your childhood

memory, and think back to the boy or girl who humiliated you at the seventh grade dinner dance. Make this person the subject of a character sketch, and vent all of your unresolved frustration into the writing. Use fiction as an outlet to settle the score. Just don't forget to change the names!

Write a story about
a con artist. How does
he choose his victims?
Has he ever suffered
a crisis of conscience?

Do your answers
change if he is a she?

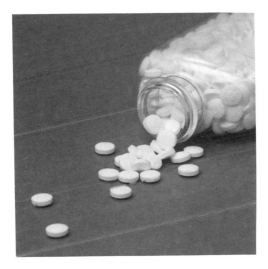

Stress

Should You Self-Publish?

As an editor, I'm often approached by authors who consider self-publishing their books, and I always advise against this (for too many reasons to list here—but, for starters, it's nearly impossible to distribute a self-published novel in the major chains like Borders that dominate the bookstore market). But other editors would disagree with me (especially in light of new "lightning press" technology), and there have been plenty of writers who self-published in the past. Robert James Waller self-published *The Bridges of Madison County*; it was noticed by Warner Books and went on to sell 6.5 mil-

lion copies. Roddy Doyle self-published his first novel, *The Commitments*, in Ireland, and it was distributed in the United States by Vintage Books, a division of Random House. Beatrix Potter self-published *The Tales of Peter Rabbit*. Stephen Crane, Virginia Woolf, Charlotte Brontë, and Marcel Proust all self-published at some point in their careers. But, I still think your energy is better spent writing new books (instead of financing, marketing, and hand-selling your old ones).

If you could script the plot
for the dream you'll have
tonight, what would it be?

Protest

Pseudonyms

Lots of writers take comfort in writing under an assumed name—and by concealing *your* identity with a pseudonym, you might feel more liberated (and less self-conscious) when writing about personal matters. Anne Rice's real name is Howard Allen O'Brien, but she uses the names A.N. Roquelaure and Anne Rampling for writing erotic fiction. Alice Rosenblum chose her pseudonym, Ayn Rand, partly to honor her Remington Rand typewriter. Ultra-prolific authors like Joyce Carol Oates and Stephen King have used their pen names, Rosamond Smith and Richard

Bachman, to avoid flooding the markets. And before finding his niche in suspense fiction, Dean Koontz used about a dozen different aliases while trying his hand at different genres (he was John Hill for writing science fiction, Leigh Nichols while writing romantic suspense and so on).

Invent a pseudonym for yourself, and then write a few pages that are markedly different in tone, style, voice, and genre from anything you've ever done. Or write the jacket flap biography about the "life" of your new persona.

Write a dialogue
between a
radio talk show
host and a
troubled caller.

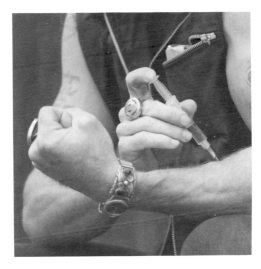

Addiction

The Perfect Lie

"The poet is a liar who always speaks the truth." So said the French filmmaker Jean Cocteau, but this definition applies to fiction writers as well. After all, the processes of telling lies and writing stories are remarkably similar. Consider the last time you overslept, and showed up two hours late for work. As you hurried to your office, your mind raced to concoct an excuse. First you ruled out anything too implausible, like earthquakes or flash floods. And once you settled on a credible story (i.e. "My car wouldn't start."), you began to fine tune your delivery, adding or embel-

lishing details along the way ("The carburetor on my Honda is totally shot. That car's been nothing but headaches since I drove it off the lot!"). Upon arriving at your job, you might even "practice" the story on a few close friends, just as you might share an early draft with members of a writing group.

Write about the worst lie you've ever gotten away with. Was it spontaneous or planned? Why did you lie? And what might have happened if the truth were discovered?

Every year, more than four hundred Americans are injured or killed by lightning.

Write about one of them.

Adoption

Tidy Up Your Desk

With its origins in Chinese tradition, Feng Shui (pronounced *fung-shway*) is the practice of living harmoniously with the energy of the surrounding environment. By moving and positioning objects within a room, feng shui teaches that we can adjust the room's energy flow. And if that sounds too "out there" for you, consider that everyone from Donald Trump to Merill Lynch and Universal Studios have employed feng shui consultants to improve the energy in their workspaces.

So why not apply four basic principals of Feng Shui to your work area? First, eliminate

all traces of clutter—file away those rejection slips, and resist the temptation to keep fifteen dog-eared revisions of your manuscript. Second, eliminate all broken or otherwise useless objects, like leaky pens and mangled paperclips. Third, make sure that 50% of your walls and work area are clear—this "white space" represents the vast potential of your future. Fourth and finally, be sure to love everything you have. Even if these ideas don't make you a better writer, you'll certainly be neater, more organized, and happier!

Write about a childhood
experience that
made you cry.

Hate

spark word

John Kennedy Toole's reputation rests on a single novel, *A Confederacy of Dunces*, which was rejected by so many publishers that the author finally committed suicide at the age of thirty-two. His mother discovered the manuscript and, in 1976, brought it to novelist Walter Percy, who was teaching at Loyola College. Looking back, Percy remembers, "[I]f ever there was something I didn't want to do, this was surely it; to deal with the mother of a dead novelist and, worst of all, to have to read a manuscript that she said was great, and that, as it turned out, was a badly smeared, scarcely readable carbon." Much to his surprise, however, Percy

loved the novel, and he helped the author's mother to find a publisher for it. Finally, in 1981, more than ten years after it was written, *A Confederacy of Dunces* was awarded the Pulitzer Prize. Moral of the story? Don't sweat over those rejection slips.

Write about a moment in your life when you've demonstrated perseverance or resilience; describe a goal that you fought to achieve, and then share the outcome of your struggle.

Imagine what life would be like if you had the occupation you'd wanted as a child.

Vacation

Inside and Out

A few years back, I met with a lawyer who was in the middle of writing a suspense thriller. She'd sent me a few chapters, which I enjoyed, and I agreed to meet her for lunch. It was a fun conversation, and at the end of the meal, when she opened her wallet to give me her business card, a small photograph fluttered out and dropped to the floor. I saw it was a picture of a woman smoking a cigarette, cut from a Virginia Slims magazine advertisement. "Do you know this person?" I asked. Blushing, the writer explained that it was Mercedes Naylor, the protagonist of her suspense novel-

in-progress. It turns out that she combed through magazines, newspapers, and catalogs to find photographs of all her characters, which she used as aids while writing her stories. She kept these pictures in her wallet, because she did a great deal of writing on Long Island railroad commuter trains.

Try this method yourself. Flip through magazines and find photographs of your characters. Or choose a photograph of someone who intrigues you, and begin a new story about this person.

According to the
Texas Department
of Transportation, one
person is killed every
year while painting
stripes on that state's
roads and highways.

Describe one of
these accidents.

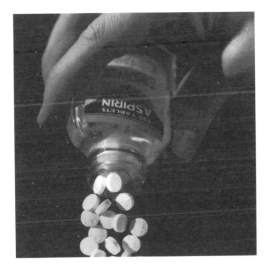

Hangover

Real People

Writers of historical fiction love to play with the restraints (and possibilities!) of past events, and frequently employ real-life figures as primary or secondary characters within their stories. In his novel *Water Music*, T.C. Boyle paired Mungo Park, a real-life Scottish explorer, with one of his fictional creations, the con artist Ned Rise. In the bestselling thriller *The Alienist*, Caleb Carr had his characters rub shoulders with real-life people like Teddy Roosevelt and J.P. Morgan. In E.L. Doctorow's *Ragtime*, we meet celebrated figures like Henry Ford, Harry Houdini, and

Sigmund Freud. And Don DeLillo's *Libra* offers illuminating portraits of everyone allegedly connected with the assassination of John F. Kennedy, from Jack Ruby to Lee Harvey Oswald.

Write about a historical era that intrigues you. Or create a scene or story that features any of the following people as primary or secondary characters: Orson Welles, Dorothy Parker, Alfred Hitchcock, Billie Holiday, Ernest Hemingway, Marilyn Monroe, or Frank Sinatra.

Write about the most difficult phone
call you've ever had to make.

Cloning

spark word

Experimenting with Tone

So a string walks into a bar and the bartender says, "I'm sorry, we don't serve strings here." The string walks back outside, rolls around in the street, and then twists itself so many times that it gets dizzy. Finally the string staggers back inside. The bartender says, "Hey, aren't you the same string that just left?" And the string replies, "No, I'm a frayed knot."

To experiment with tone, rewrite this story as it might be told by any of the following four people: a stand-up comedian, a prime-time news reporter, an evangelical minister, or a gangster rapper. In each instance, the plot will

remain the same, but each narrator will add or embellish details to suit his or her own personal needs. A bad stand-up comedian might punctuate the joke with profanity in a desperate attempt for laughs. A news reporter might spin the tale as another example of racial discrimination. Play around with these until you find a voice that intrigues you.

Describe the most unusual cure or home remedy you've ever tried.

Border

spark word

Ask Questions

When Vladimir Nabokov visited Penn State University in the 1970s, he took a walking tour of the campus with several creative writing students. At one point, Nabokov pointed to a tree and asked what its name was. None of the students could answer him, even though there were dozens of the same tree all across campus. So Nabokov asked, "How can you all expect to be writers and not know the names of the trees in your own country?"

Fiction writers need the instincts of a good reporter. Start asking questions. Learn as much as you can. If you find yourself sitting

next to a brain surgeon on an airplane flight, make the most of the opportunity and start up a conversation. Relish the opportunity to attend parties where you don't know anyone. Read widely and extensively about subjects you don't understand. Take a subject at random—aviation, zoology, anything—and immerse yourself in its minutiae. The more you know about the world, the more you'll want to write about it.

Write about a dream or
a goal that you failed
to achieve. What went
wrong? And how did the
experience change you?

Aphrodisiac

Distance Yourself

Many experiences lend themselves to fiction immediately—we incorporate everyday happenings and observations into our stories all the time. But some events require more distance before a writer can fully understand them. Literary agent Ann Rittenberg once told me about one of her clients, a woman who had published a first novel to glowing reviews. Soon after its publication, however, the author's father committed suicide, and the author decided to make his death the subject of her second novel. The task proved to be impossible—after years of false starts and

dead ends, she eventually abandoned the project and moved on to something else. "She was too close to the experience," Rittenberg told me. "With any kind of major life experience or tragedy, it takes time to make sense of them."

If you're stuck in the middle of a story, consider how much distance is between yourself and the subject matter. Do you understand it now? Could you write the story with more understanding or clarity five years from now?

Describe the clearest,

most vivid memory

of your childhood—

a moment that has

stayed with you all

of your life.

Extinction

Analyze Your Characters

E.L. Doctorow once described the novelist as "a person who lives in other people's skins." If you've hit a snag in your writing, the majority of problems can usually be solved by returning to the question of character. Tom McCormack, the former Publisher of St. Martin's Press and editor of such novels as *The Silence of the Lambs*, would advise authors to ask six questions of their characters: What does the character want? What does he or she do to get it? What is the result? Why should the reader care? How does the character conflict or braid with others? And how is it resolved at the end?

If you're suffering from writer's block, ask these six questions about each of the principles in *your* fiction. And when you're finished, perhaps you'll continue asking questions. As W. Somerset Maugham once remarked, "You can never know enough about your characters."

Check the horoscope
in today's newspaper,

and use any of the
twelve forecasts as the
basis for a character.

Casualty

spark word

Read a Celebrity Memoir

Ah, the celebrity memoir—a comforting reminder that good writing has very little to do with getting published. Consider *Monica's Story*, the authorized bio of White House intern Monica Lewinsky, which skyrocketed up bestseller lists despite such clunky lines as, "Like blood seeping out from under a closed door, the awful truth began to dawn." In *The Dogg Father*, gangsta rapper Snoop Doggy Dogg ponders a number of existential conundrums like this one: "Chances are that most of the brothers on the block are homies you knew on the street, and out on the street most of the

homies you hang with are brothers you knew on the block." Finally, in *If Only*, former Spice Girl Geri Halliwell demonstrates her newfound maturity while trying on a dress that doesn't quite fit. "The old Geri would have tried to squeeze into the smaller size, but instead I chose the next size up. For me this was an important step towards self-acceptance."

Now that you've seen a few examples, write a page or so in the voice of your favorite overexposed celebrity.

Describe the unhealthiest meal
you've ever eaten—and how
you felt after eating it.

Opening Night

Dialect

The *Adventures of Huckleberry Finn* has probably inspired thousands of writers to try their hand at writing in dialect, but very few of them have done the job as well as Mark Twain (who gave the runaway slave Jim long passages of dialogue with lines like this: "I see light a-comin' roun' de p'int, bymeby, so I wade' in en shove' a log ahead o' me, en swum more'n halfway acrost de river . . .").

That's *good* dialect. *Bad* dialect is what you read In cheesy vampire stories ("I *vant* to *zuck* your *bluhd*") and third rate Westerns ("Buenos dias, Meestah Smeeth! You like dee girls? Dees

girls are preety fine, *señor*—"). Novelist and creative writing instructor Anne Lamott often cautions her students about the risks of writing dialect: "[B]e positive that you do it well, because otherwise it is a lot of work to read short stories or a novel that are written in dialect. It makes our necks feel funny."

Dialect *is* difficult, but give it a shot anyway. Model your character after someone you know personally, and you'll be less likely to end up with language that is stereotyped.

Think back to the last person you saw with a physical disability. Imagine what they're doing right now.

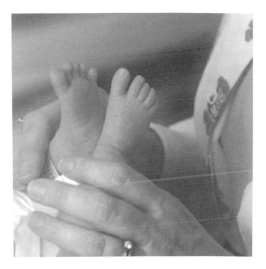

Midwife

Start at the End

Strange as it may seem, there are plenty of writers who begin a story by writing the ending. Katherine Anne Porter once said, "If I didn't know the ending of a story, I wouldn't begin. I always write my last lines, my last paragraph, my last page first." Toni Morrison agrees with her: "I always start a novel by writing its first page and its last page, which seem to survive almost intact through all the following drafts and changes." By writing your ending first, you'll actually have to "backtrack" through character and story development—a useful exercise for any fiction writer, if you've

never tried it. Another helpful idea is to review the endings of your favorite novels and determine what makes them effective. Do they conclude with grand declarations of love? Climactic courtroom accusations? Subtle, metaphoric observations? Figure out why these final moments work, and then start *your* next story by writing the end first.

Write a
description of
your dream
automobile.

Insanity

Expand Your Toolbox

Elsewhere in *The Writer's Block*, you'll find suggestions for tackling stories in the form of screenplays and poetry. But both of these alternatives still require you to work with language—and that may or may not be the best approach, depending on how well you understand your subject matter. Perhaps you're unsure of characters but know the general theme you want to explore. Or maybe you haven't nailed down a plot or setting, but really want to delve into a certain emotion or conflict. In instances like these, it can help to begin in a media that doesn't depend on lan-

guage—think painting, drawing, collage, sculpture, woodworking, even music and dance. Use any one of these creative outlets as a means for exploring your ideas. Draw the house in which your main character grew up. Express his or her frustrations in a blaze of interpretive dance. Strum an acoustic guitar as you mull over their unrealized dreams and ambitions. By embracing the tools of other media, you'll prepare yourself for the process of developing your ideas in fiction.

Roadkill

spark word

Write a story that begins with an explosion.

on Writing" series, in which contemporary novelists discuss their craft). Best of all, it's absolutely free.

Atlantic Monthly Unbound (www.atlanticmonthly): Another fabulous, fabulous site. Next time you read an excellent short story in *The Atlantic Monthly*, go straight to this website and you'll find an interview with the author that goes behind-the-scenes to discuss the genesis of the work. Also available are book reviews, poetry pages, and much more—the end result is a worthy electronic supplement to a terrific magazine.

Salon (www.salonmagazine.com/books): This internet-only magazine publishes many of the freshest voices in contemorary writing, so it's no surprise

The Atlantic Monthly
The Paris Review
The Writer
Writer's Digest
The New York Times
The San Francisco Chronicle

General Websites:

The New York Times (www.nytimes.com/books):
It doesn't get any better than this. For starters, you can search more than fifty thousand book reviews published in *The New York Times* since 1980. Also on hand are first chapters from hundreds of novels, plus zillions of articles by or about great authors (look for the "Writers

Infectious

Tom Wolfe gave his first public reading of *A Man in Full* to a sold-out crowd at New York City's Town Hall, and he began the night with a few words about sourcing inspiration: "I have a somewhat unusual approach to writing novels. Most writers look first for a theme and probably a character who three out of four times is themselves. Instead—maybe it's the journalist in me, it probably is—I look for a milieu, a setting that to me is fascinating and a setting I don't know anything about." In the case of *A Man in Full*, the setting was the city and surroundings of Atlanta, Georgia, but John Berendt accomplished a similar feat with *Midnight in the Garden of Good and Evil*,

Surprise

spark word

Create a character
who is struggling
with writer's block.

Steinberg, Sybil, ed. *Writing for Your Life.*
New York: Pushcart Press, 1992. Derived from a
long-running series of interviews from *Publisher's
Weekly*, this collection features ninety-two
contemporary authors discussing the pleasures
and agonies of the writing life.

Winokur, Jon, ed. *Advice to Writers.* New York:
Pantheon, 1999. Like Winokur's earlier
Writers on Writing (currently out of print), this
volume is chock full of carefully selected
quotations from more than four hundred
celebrated authors.

Newspapers and Periodicals:
Publisher's Weekly

excerpts from nearly fifty years of interviews with subjects like Hemingway, Frost, Pound, Eliot, and Forster. This is easily the best $19.95 you'll ever spend. (If you're short on cash, return *The Writer's Block* to your bookstore, beg for a refund, and buy *The Writer's Chapbook* instead. You need it more.)

Schwartz, Ronald B. *For the Love of Books*. New York: Putnam, 1999. More than one hundred distinguished writers—from Diane Ackerman to Tobias Wolf—respond to the question: What books have left the greatest impression on you and why?

Stein, Sol. *Stein on Writing*. New York, St. Martin's Press, 1995.

THE WRITER'S THE WRITER'S

BLOCK BLOCK

by Jason Rekulak

RUNNING PRESS

786 IDEAS TO JUMP-START YOUR IMAGINATION

Bibliography

While researching *The Writer's Block*, I consulted hundreds of newspapers, magazines, books, and websites; the best of these sources are highlighted on the next few pages. If you're interested in reading more about writing, these publications are an excellent place to further your education.

Books:
Ash, Russell and Lake, Brian. *Bizarre Books.*
   London: Pavilion, 1998.
Bernard, André. *Now All We Need is a Title.*
   New York: Norton, 1994.

Blythe, Will, ed. *Why I Write*. New York: Little, Brown and Company, 1998. Blythe posed the simple question—"Why do you write?"—to twenty-six contemporary fiction writers, including Rick Bass, Pat Conroy, Mary Gaitskill, Thom Jones, and others. Through essay-length responses, these writers illuminate the motivation behind their work.

Bradbury, Ray. *Zen in the Art of Writing*. Santa Barbara: Capra Press, 1989.

Brande, Dorothea. *Becoming a Writer*. Los Angeles: J.P. Tarcher, 1981. First published in 1934, this much-loved book eschews traditional creative writing instruction and focuses instead on problems of confidence, self-respect, and personal freedom.

Burnham, Sophy. *For Writers Only*. New York: Ballantine, 1994.

Busch, Frederick, ed. *Letters to a Fiction Writer*. New York: Norton, 1999. Letters of advice from novelists to aspiring writers, with contributions from Anne Beattie, John Updike, Raymond Carver, Flannery O'Connor, and others.

Canfield, Jack and Hansen, Mark Victor and Gardner, Bud, eds. *Chicken Soup for the Writer's Soul*. Deerfield Beach. Heath Communications, 2000.

Epel, Naomi. *Writers Dreaming*. New York: Crown, 1994.

Gardner, John. *The Art of Fiction*. New York: Knopf, 1983.

Glossbrenner, Alfred and Emily. *About the Author.* New York: Harcourt, 2000. Lively and intelligent profiles of 125 beloved fiction authors—everyone from Jane Austen to Don DeLillo and Danielle Steel—with plenty of juicy tidbits (if you want to know why Norman Mailer stabbed his second wife with a "dirty three-inch penknife," look no further).

Goldberg, Natalie. *Writing Down the Bones.* Boston: Shambhala, 1986.

Henderson, Bill and Bernard, André, eds. *Pushcart's Complete Rotten Reviews and Rejections.* New York: Pushcart Press, 1998.

Krementz, Jill. *The Writer's Desk.* New York: Random House, 1996.

Lamott, Anne. *Bird by Bird*. New York: Pantheon, 1994.

Malone, Aubrey Dillon. *Stranger than Fiction*. Chicago: Contemporary Books, 2000.

Neubauer, Alexander. *Conversations on Writing Fiction*. New York: HarperPerennial, 1994. Although out-of-print, it's worth tracking down if you've ever considered enrolling in an MFA program. *Conversations* features interviews with thirteen distinguished teachers of creative writing, including T.C. Boyle, Rosellen Brown, John Irving, Gordon Lish, and Jane Smiley.

Plimpton, George, ed. *The Writer's Chapbook*. New York: The Modern Library, 1999. This must-have volume compiles the most memorable

THE WRITER'S

BLOCK